WILDFLOWERS OF THE TALLGRASS PRAIRIE

WILDFLOWERS
OF THE TALLGRASS PRAIRIE:
THE UPPER MIDWEST

BY SYLVAN T. RUNKEL AND DEAN M. ROOSA

WITH A FOREWORD BY JOHN MADSON

IOWA STATE UNIVERSITY PRESS  AMES

SYLVAN T. RUNKEL, best known as "Sy," was the senior natural historian of Iowa. He had a special skill in communicating with people of all ages on the importance of woodlands and prairies. He spent a lifetime interpreting nature to groups, assisting in workshops, lecturing, serving on boards and committees, saving endangered habitats, and developing outdoor classrooms and nature trails, gently gaining supporters of natural areas.

Even in retirement, Sy was much in demand for programs on natural history, for service on boards and committees, and for work with conservation groups. He served as president of the Iowa chapters of the Soil Conservation Society of America, the Society of American Foresters, and the Wildlife Society. As chairman of the State Preserves Advisory Board and board member of The Nature Conservancy, he was instrumental in preserving many natural areas.

His awards and honors are numerous—Iowa Conservationist of the Year, Federal Civil Servant of the Year, Iowa Conservation Hall of Fame, The Nature Conservancy's Oak Leaf Award, Frudden Award of the Iowa Chapter of the Society of American Foresters, and the Silver Beaver Award from the Boy Scouts of America. He was also a fellow of the Iowa Academy of Science, the Soil Conservation Society of America, and the Society of American Foresters.

Except for 5 years as a glider pilot in World War II, the thrust of his 40 years with the federal government (mostly Soil Conservation Service) was conservation.

Sy, along with Alvin F. Bull, wrote *Wildflowers of Iowa Woodlands, Wildflowers of Illinois Woodlands,* and *Wildflowers of Indiana Woodlands.*

DEAN M. ROOSA has served as State Ecologist for Iowa since 1975. He is employed by the Department of Natural Resources to work with the State Preserves Advisory Board, a seven-member board appointed by the governor to establish a system of state preserves. His activities include recommending sites to the Board for formal dedication by the governor.

Dean has served as board member of the Iowa Chapter of The Nature Conservancy, board member of the Natural Areas Association, chairman of the Iowa Natural History Association, and president of the Iowa Ornithologists' Union. He has been awarded Distinguished Service Awards from the Iowa Academy of Science and from The Nature Conservancy and was given an honorary Doctor of Science degree from Grinnell College in 1982.

His master's thesis at the University of Northern Iowa was in ornithology, and his doctoral dissertation at Iowa State University was in wetland ecology. His principal research interests are raptor biology and wetland ecology. He is one of the authors of *Iowa Birds* and of *Iowa's Natural Heritage.*

Prior to his service as State Ecologist, he was a high school science teacher for 14 years.

He lives in a rural area near Ames, Iowa.

First edition, 1989
Second printing, 1989
Third printing, 1992
Fourth printing, 1994
Fifth printing, 1996

Library of Congress Cataloging-in-Publication Data
Runkel, Sylvan T.
    Wildflowers of the tallgrass prairie: the upper Midwest / by Sylvan T. Runkel and Dean M. Roosa: with a foreword by John Madson.—1st ed.
        p.   cm.
    Bibliography: p.
    Includes index.
    ISBN 0-8138-1979-2
    1. Wildflowers—Middle West. 2. Wildflowers—Middle West—Identification. I. Roosa, Dean M. II. Title.
QK128.R86   1989
582.13'0977—dc19   87-34482

Cover photo courtesy of Carl Kurtz

DEDICATION: To Alvin F. Bull, who hoped to see a book on prairie wildflowers published. Al coauthored three books on woodland wildflowers and was the intended coauthor of this book. He was assembling information on prairie wildflowers when he died unexpectedly. To him and to the fulfillment of his dream, we respectfully dedicate this book.

CONTENTS

Tallgrass prairie is a bittersweet thing.

In deep winter when the long winds blow out of the northwest, the prairie world can be as cold, hard, and cheerless as iron—a bitter place of wind-packed snow and of sere and broken stems, a colorless monotony of white, gray, and dun. Long ago, Washington Irving wrote: "To one unaccustomed to it, there is something inexpressibly lonely in the solitude of the prairie. The loneliness of a forest seems nothing to it." If the human emotion of loneliness can be defined as a bleak desolation of spirit—a sort of gray hopelessness unrelieved by any color or joy—then winter prairie is surely one of its embodiments.

And then, suddenly, all that begins to change. Sometime in the night, perhaps, a spring chinook begins to blow and the hard winter winds shift and soften. The annual prairie miracle is under way. The lonely time begins to pass. Company is coming. There is a rich, loamy sweetness to the air as the sun warms the deep prairie soils and life begins to emerge from winter hiding. A faint wash of green appears on the gray-dun prairie landscape and then, on some fine day in late April or early May, the first real splashes of floral pigments are added. From then until hard frost, there will be no time when the prairie is without flowers. In wave after wave of floral successions in indigo, pale lavender, crimson, gold, cream, white, and magenta—in every tone and hue of the artist's palette—the prairie flowers come on. For 6 months or more the rich and varied panorama will continue, changing from week to week, beginning with ground-hugging pasque flowers and birdsfoot violets and climaxing with towering sunflowers. Many of their names are pure Americana: rattlesnake master, bundleflower, compass plant, prairie smoke, cowboy's delight, lousewort, spiderwort, New Jersey tea, queen-of-the-prairie, shooting star, blazing star, alumroot, blue-eyed grass, yellow star-grass, bellflower, windflower, bastard toadflax, prairie gayfeather, butterfly milkweed, and button snakeroot.

All of these, and more, are carefully and lovingly treated in the following pages by Sylvan Runkel and Dean Roosa, a pair of long-time prairie ramblers who know the tallgrass country and the native flowers to be found there. They have included certain tallgrasses as well, since these comprise the setting in which prairie flowers are displayed. And although this book was written in Iowa by a team of Iowans, the flowers shown here are typical of most tallgrass prairie country of the North American heartland.

Some are still fairly common field flowers and will be familiar to many who read this book. Those flowers are the hardy natives that have managed the crucial shift from native grassland to tame roadsides, fallow pastures, and some urban weed patches. Although we are likely to take them for granted, and even treat some with the contempt we seem to reserve for those native plants and animals that manage to thrive in our dreariest habitats, they are not less beautiful for being commonplace.

Some of the other flowers shown in this book are fading from modern memory. Too fragile to live away from quality tallgrass prairie, they are "decreasers" that cannot survive heavy grazing, incessant mowing, or the breaking of the deep, infinitely complex prairie soils to which they have adapted. Some are great showy blooms; others are small secret blossoms, as rare and solitary as jewels, that may be trod upon without being noticed. But common or rare, showy or not, the flowers of the tallgrass prairies are best seen in their own frame of native grasses, lit by the lofty vault of prairie sky; as that setting fades, so does the real meaning of its blossoms.

Native tallgrass prairie is still the rarest of all major North American biomes. However, no aspect of environmental awareness is sharper or more vigorous than concern for tallgrass prairie. The preservation and restoration of our tall grasslands has become a citizen conservation effort of the first rank—and not a day too soon. Some of this concern may be due to our typical American sympathy for the underdog (with a measure of guilt thrown in), but most of the rising interest in native prairie has come from a greater understanding of what quality native landscapes really are and of what they really mean. That understanding is the last, best hope for such places as redwood groves, wild seashores, alpine meadows, rich marshlands, and native tallgrass prairie. It may even be one of our own best hopes of happiness.

JOHN MADSON
Godfrey, Illinois

x

As the interest in prairies grew, so did the need for books and keys to aid in identifying prairie plants. This book is designed to help the interested amateur become better acquainted with the more common prairie plants; it describes mainly the wildflowers that are found on the remnant prairies of the Upper Midwest. Flower descriptions occur in the approximate order of their blooming time, although this varies somewhat throughout the tallgrass prairie and from year to year.

Common names vary so much throughout the country that we have included those in frequent use, although others may be used locally or regionally. Because a common name may be applied to more than one species, we have in each case included the plant's Latin name, along with the authority.

While knowledge of this two-name system of naming plants is not necessary for the enjoyment of the prairie, the system is both useful and practical. The first name, the genus name (plural: genera), applies to a group of closely related species. The family name (for example, Rosaceae) indicates groupings of closely related genera. The scientific name, usually derived from Latin or Greek, is often descriptive of the plant. This helps the prairie enthusiast remember the name of the plant, and conversely, by observing the plant, one may be able to recall the scientific name.

Some of the species included may be as much at home on the woodland edge as on the prairie. Indeed, some may shift their habitat preference in different parts of the tallgrass prairie biome. In certain parts of the biome, a few species may be regarded more as weeds than true prairie plants.

We hope the pictures, contributed by a host of photographers from throughout the Midwest, coupled with the interesting bits of information about the plants will increase the enjoyment of the prairie visitor. We especially hope teachers may gain the confidence to visit these priceless remnants with their classes. To enhance interest, we have included information on how these plants were used by native Americans and early pioneers. The spelling of native American names is as we found them recorded by the early botanists, physicians, and herbalists.

Please remember that prairies can be miserably hot places with no shade for an escape. Prairies can abound with chiggers and other insects, and poison ivy can be abundant in some prairies, especially those close to a woodland. But they can also be among the most peaceful places on earth if visited early, before the sun becomes punishing, or late, when the wind has died with the setting sun.

ACKNOWLEDGMENTS

Encouragement for compiling a book of this nature has come from many persons: professional botanists, enthusiastic amateurs, naturalists—all wonderful friends of the authors. Such encouragement is essential and appreciated, and we take this opportunity to express our sincere gratitude.

We thank the professionals who reviewed the manuscript: Don Farrar, Iowa State University; Bill Pusateri, Des Moines; and Jim Peck, University of Arkansas, Little Rock. Their comments were helpful and appreciated. Special thanks to Ida Ruth Miller for proofreading and to Mr. and Mrs. LeRoy Pratt, Des Moines, who graciously agreed to assist in proofreading and in preparing an index. The following people helped in estimating the amount of remaining prairie: Bob Djupstrom, Bonnie Heidel, Mike Homoya, Don Kurz, John Pearson, John Schwegman, Bill Smith, Curt Twedt, and James H. Wilson.

We especially thank Debbie McRae, who spent considerable time editing the text to ensure that the information is both accurate and easily understood. Debbie is the daughter of the late Alvin Bull, coauthor of *Wildflowers of Iowa Woodlands*.

A very special thanks goes to Carol Bull for her unending encouragement and support even in the face of the sudden tragic loss of her husband.

DISCLAIMER

We often highlight the historical use of various prairie plants for medicinal or nutritive purposes. For obvious reasons we do *not* recommend plants be used for these purposes today. First, the identity of the plant is not always assured; second, there are drastically fewer prairie plants today than historically; third, the method of treatment using plants was purely trial-and-error and surely resulted in many unfortunate incidents; fourth, tolerance to a plant product varies markedly from person to person; finally, the long time period and method of translation of information involved could make any information available less than fully accurate. It is far better to enjoy the plants in their native habitat—that is our recommendation.

WILDFLOWERS OF THE TALLGRASS PRAIRIE

What is this thing called *prairie?* If one characteristic must be listed, it would be the domination by grasses: they define the prairie as surely as trees define the forest. The major grasses are big bluestem, Indian grass, switchgrass, porcupine grass, June grass, sand reed, and slough grass. Throw in 25 or so more grasses and some 250 forbs that love the open sun — and you have the beginning of a prairie. Now add a dozen small mammals, 20 or so species of birds, hundreds of invertebrates, scores of nematodes, bacteria, lichens, and mosses — and you have a more complete prairie. Give it hundreds of years to develop, some large herbivores and carnivores, and all the respect you can muster — and you may finally have the semblance of a prairie. Now add raging prairie fires to maintain the grassy integrity, for without fires, you will soon have a young forest because today's climate favors the growth of trees. These fires, so much a part of our natural world prior to settlement, have been suppressed for the past century by human activities. Controlled fires are now a standard part of prairie management, and nearly all prairie remnants in the Upper Midwest are annually burned, cut for hay, or grazed.

There are a variety of types of prairie in the Upper Midwest. They range from the blacksoil prairies, those with the deep black loam where grasses grow higher than one's head, to the sand plains, where grasses and forbs sparsely populate the open sand. In between are hill prairies, existing on steep hillsides that have a thin soil over bedrock; loess prairies, often existing on steep loess hillslopes where grazing is difficult and farming impossible; and gravel prairies, existing on ridges of gravel left by the retreating glacier. All are within the boundaries of the tallgrass prairie biome, with mixed-grass prairie bordering it on the west and with shortgrass prairie still farther west.

THE BEGINNING

The tallgrass prairie biome extends from southernmost Manitoba south to Texas and from eastern Nebraska to Indiana (Risser et al. 1981), with disjunct sites east into Ohio (Transeau 1935) (see Figure 1). The original tallgrass prairie is estimated to have covered an area of 573,511 sq. km. (221,436 sq. mi.), about the same amount covered by mixed-grass prairie (Risser et al. 1981).

The tallgrass prairie was not always this vast; it expanded rather dramatically during a period of warm, dry climate, the "xerothermic" or "hypsithermal," which favored the development and expansion of prairie. This warm period lasted about 5000

Figure 1. Approximate extent of the tallgrass prairie region at the time of settlement. (*Adapted from Risser et al. 1981 and Transeau 1935. Map prepared by Larry Pool and Carol Peck.*)

years—from 8000 to 3000 years ago. Then a cool, moist climate returned, favoring the expansion of forest.

For millennia the prairie knew grazing bison, the sweep of prairie fires across the plains, and ferocious winter blizzards; but, seemingly undisturbed, its multitude of grasses and forbs slowly built the richest legacy of black soil known to man. This was accomplished by the slow incorporation of decaying plants into the humus with the help of an array of soil invertebrates, fungi, and bacteria. The result was a thick prairie soil capped with sod so tough that the pioneers despaired of ever turning it to expose the black topsoil, especially with oxen and the wooden plow.

THE END

Given the vast extent of the prairie and the toughness of the sod, the end came with surprising suddenness. With the invention of the steel moldboard plow by John Deere in 1837, it became possible to turn the sod with ease. Basically, by 1860 the tallgrass prairie, particularly in Illinois, Indiana, Ohio, and Iowa, was no more. Ironically, the very richness of these prairie soils was their greatest liability. With rapid and steady advance, the richest prairies became the most bountiful of croplands.

Estimates have been made that 1 percent of the original prairie survived; however, that figure was compiled before most states sponsored research to discover and document remnant prairies. In the Upper Midwest, less than 1 percent remains; in the lower drainages of the Missouri and Mississippi rivers, considerably more than 1 percent remains. In Iowa, if the Loess Hills in western Iowa are considered mixed-grass prairie, perhaps fewer than 10,000 acres, only 3000 to 4000 of which are relatively undamaged by human activities, are extant. Illinois has fewer than 1300 acres of high quality prairies remaining; Indiana, not more than a few hundred acres; Minnesota, 75,000 to 150,000 acres, ranging from high quality to severely degraded; Missouri, perhaps 70,000 acres; North Dakota, fewer than 2000 acres; South Dakota, about 50,000 acres of rangeland in good to excellent condition; Wisconsin, about 4000 acres, but this includes the oak savannas; and Nebraska, less than 2 percent of the tallgrass prairie. In the western portion of the tallgrass prairie biome, lower rainfall and thin, rocky soils prevail. Although much of this prairie has not been plowed, it has been affected by decades of grazing.

THE RESURGENCE

In approximately the past two decades, many people have become interested in the tallgrass prairies. Perhaps we suddenly realized how much we had lost — and what a miracle we had lost.

This resurgence of interest and activity includes innumerable restoration projects, prairie symposia, the North American Prairie Conference, and the celebration of prairie week in various states. The amount of literature and books published about prairies and the number of businesses specializing in selling prairie seeds, books, and information on prairies has increased. Many states have begun to inventory the remnant prairies and some states have instituted "registry" programs designed to provide an interim form of protection.

CONSERVATION

Some of the more delicate and sensitive prairie plants have been driven to the edge of extinction by the near destruction of the tallgrass prairie. Fortunately, we may have learned to care in time to save representative samples of this mighty ecosystem. There is a great need to learn about the basic biology of these plants so we can develop protective strategies for them. We still know so little of the total ecology of the prairie biome; for example, we are only now beginning to understand the association of butterflies and prairie plants. Soil microbes are virtually unstudied.

Nearly every state in the tallgrass biome has a system of areas for scientific study (called various names from state to state). State-funded boards, working in concert with state Departments of Natural Resources, have provided impetus for prairie protection. Some states have very effective County Conservation Boards, which have become a driving force in prairie preservation.

Private nonprofit organizations such as The Nature Conservancy, the Missouri Prairie Foundation, the Iowa Natural Heritage Foundation, the Illinois Natural Land Institute, and the Grassland Heritage Foundation have been instrumental in saving prairies. It is gratifying that when people inventory a given state, they find prairies existing in out-of-the-way places that were difficult to plow, along railroads, and in cemeteries, and they occasionally find a prairie that was set aside purely for the enjoyment of the wildflowers.

These discoveries need to be followed by landowner contacts, since often the owner, once informed of the special nature of the prairie, is eager to see that it is protected. It seems evident that segments of this once-extensive ecosystem should be preserved as a living laboratory for the soil scientist who may want to study the virgin soil profile after erosion has taken its toll on the cultivated landscape.

As the prairie goes, so go its dependents; and the first to go are those species with naturally small populations, those with large ranges that compete with humans for space, and those with very narrow ecological tolerance. This is why the bison is gone and why large herbivores are in trouble; this is why the whooping crane has left the prairie biome; this is why many prairie plants are at the edge of extinction.

Can you imagine a world without a Northern Harrier coursing a prairie, without a Short-eared Owl performing its courtship flights, without the haunting call of the Curlew, without the beauty of the prairie fringed orchid? Our generation may be the last to have the opportunity to ensure a world with these sights and sounds in it. If the prairie goes, an entire natural community is lost forever—a community that was the foundation of our midwestern society. Perhaps the present interest in prairies will mean a more enduring relationship with our basis of life: the natural environment.

Other common names: April fool, badger, Easter plant, gosling, hartshorn, prairie smoke (also applied to another plant), rock lily, wild crocus, windflower

Anemone: the ancient Greek and Latin name, a variation of the Semitic name for the mythological Adonis, from whose blood a crimson-flowered *Anemone* of the Orient is said to have sprung

Patens: from Latin, meaning "spreading"

Buttercup family: Ranunculaceae

Found in dry prairies from the Arctic to the southern United States. The earliest of prairie flowers, it blooms in March and April.

Pasque flower grows 2 to 16 inches tall from a brownish perennial crown. The hairy, gray-green stems grow somewhat erect from a thick, horizontal rootstock.

Basal leaves, arising from the crown on long petioles, are broader than long and are somewhat kidney-shaped in overall outline. The three segments of each leaf are deeply cut into numerous linear lobes, so the appearance is somewhat fernlike. Similar but smaller leaves with petioles occur just below the flower. The leaves are covered with long, silky hairs.

A single, large, striking flower is borne at the tip of a long flowerstalk. These flowers have no true petals but have five (sometimes seven) colorful sepals. These sepals—blue, purple, or white—form a flower about 1 inch across and up to 1½ inches long. Each sepal is somewhat oval, often with a bluntly pointed tip. In the center of the flower is a yellow-orange disk.

Each seed has a long, featherlike plume. Reproduction is by these wind-dispersed seeds.

The crushed leaves of pasque flowers served American Indians as a counterirritant for the treatment of rheumatism and other painful ailments. The plant was used as a diaphoretic, a diuretic, and a rubefacient and as a treatment for boils, burns, and sore eyes. The dried, powdered plant sometimes was used to promote healing of wounds. Caution was exercised because the plant contains alkaloids that cause depression, nervousness, and an upset stomach.

This plant was on the official list of U.S. Pharmocopaea from 1882 to 1908 because of its diuretic, expectorant, and menstrual-inducing qualities. European herbalists used it to treat sterility and infected ovaries. In Europe it was once highly valued for treating nervous exhaustion that was due to various menstrual complaints. It was supposed to be most effective if taken by blue-eyed, fair-haired women.

The Dakota had a special song about the pasque flower; it essentially encouraged other flowers to follow the pasque flower in appearing soon. There was ceremonial smoking upon seeing the first pasque flower of spring; then, the flowers were picked and taken home. Songs were sung along the way, and these songs were taught to the children or grandchildren.

photograph by Randall A. Maas

Other common names: false dandelion, goat chicory, prairie false dandelion

Agoseris: from the Greek *aix* for "goat" and *seris* for "chicory"

Cuspidata: from Latin, meaning "with a cusp," a sharp and rigid point

Daisy family: Asteraceae (Compositae)

Found on dry prairies and stony hills of the Midwest and Great Plains, ranging from Wisconsin to Montana, south to Missouri, Illinois, and Oklahoma. Blooming time is April through May.

The strong, perennial taproot of prairie dandelion produces a basal tuft of grasslike leaves. These leaves are 4 to 8 inches long, less than ½ inch wide, and somewhat thick. Leaf margins tend to be woolly with fine, white hairs. The leaves also tend to fold lengthwise along the midrib.

A yellow dandelion-like flower appears early, before the prairie grasses grow tall enough to hide it. Each tops a stout, leafless stalk that may be as much as 1 foot high. Usually this flowerstalk is no longer than the longest of the plant's leaves. The flower is 1 to 2 inches across and 1 inch high. The straplike rays of the flower, distinctly five-toothed at the tip, are less numerous than those of the dandelion flower. The greenish bracts at the base of the flower are narrow and sharply pointed. The flower becomes purplish with age.

The slender, rod-shaped seeds become about ¼ inch long at maturity. Each has 10 ridges and is tipped with 40 to 50 unequal, white, bristle-like hairs. Reproduction is by these wind-dispersed seeds.

The young roots of prairie dandelion were eaten raw by early settlers on the upper Great Plains.

When tissues of *A. glauca,* a related species, are broken, they exude a milky juice that turns dark and thick on exposure to air. This solidified substance was chewed by western American Indians. It contains some rubber but not enough to be valuable.

A. glauca is a Great Plains species with dentate or laciniate leaves, a beaked achene, and a bluish cast. Taxonomists are not in agreement on the proper name for this taxon, and it is also known as *Microseris* and *Nothocalais.*

Because of its early flowering habit, prairie dandelion is a welcome sight on the early prairie landscape, often the only splash of color in an otherwise drab ridgetop.

photograph by John Schwegman

Other common names: lousewort, snaffles, beefsteak plant, high heal-all

Pedicularis: from Latin *pediculus,* meaning "louse" or "lousy." Cattle and sheep grazing in pastures with this plant were once expected to become infected with lice.

Canadensis: meaning "of Canada"

Snapdragon family: Scrophulariaceae

Found in upland soils or prairies and woodland clearings throughout the central and eastern parts of the nation, it grows best in somewhat acid soils. Flowers April to June.

Another species, *P. lanceolata,* prefers wet areas.

This perennial usually flowers when its unbranched, hairy stem is 6 to 10 inches tall, but it continues to grow as tall as 18 inches. Long, narrow leaves up to 5 inches long are deeply cut about halfway to the midrib, which gives them a fernlike appearance. Leaves along the stem are usually alternate. Petioles are present except for some leaves near the top. The leaves have a downy or fuzzy appearance and a silvery green color. Basal leaves may show a beautiful wine red color in the early spring before they turn green.

Wood betony may be partially parasitic on roots of other plants, especially grasses.

Snapdragon-like flowers nearly 1 inch long crowd in dense clusters at the top of the unbranched stem. Two distinct lips are evident. The upper lip, somewhat flattened and spreading, curves in a long arch to form a distinct hood. The lower lip, with three rounded lobes, is shorter and spreading.

Flowers are greenish yellow at first, but as the spike lengthens, the hood, or upper lip, darkens to a purplish or reddish color. The lower lip remains pale yellow. Some of the reddish, or beefsteak, color may creep into the stems and leaves as well.

The fruit capsule, about ⅔ inch long, contains several seeds.

Apparently this plant was not of major importance to American Indians and pioneers, although it had several uses. The Meskwaki and the Prairie Potawatomi boiled the whole plant to make a tea for reducing internal swellings and tumors and some types of external swelling. They also applied a poultice made from the roots to external swellings. This poultice also was used for rattlesnake bite and as a magic charm.

Several tribes used it as a love charm. The Ojibwa chopped up the root and slipped it into food that was cooking, unbeknownst to the people who were to eat it. If these people had been quarrelsome, then they would become lovers again. Medicine men were said to sometimes take advantage of its powers. The Menomini carried the root with them if they contemplated making advances of love.

The Forest Potawatomi fed a mixture of oats and the roots of this plant to their ponies to fatten them. They also used it as a physic. The Menomini believed feeding the plant to a pony made the animal vicious to all but its owner.

photograph by John Schwegman

Other common names: golden meadow parsnip

Zizia: in honor of Johann Baptist Ziz, German botanist of the late 18th and early 19th centuries

Aurea: from Latin, meaning "golden"

Parsley family: Apiaceae (Umbelliferae)

Found throughout the tallgrass prairie and elsewhere, preferring moist soils of open areas. Blooms April through June.

The smooth stem with a reddish tinge to its bright green color grows 1 to 3 feet tall. Compared to its parsnip relatives, this perennial is small and delicate. It typically has a few spreading branches. The short taproot is ½ to ¾ inch in diameter and is a yellowish color inside.

The alternate leaves are divided into three leaflets, and sometimes each of the leaflets is further subdivided into three parts. Leaves lower on the stem tend to have more leaflets. Leaflets, which are usually 1 to 2 inches long, vary from lance-shaped to egg-shaped and have toothed margins. Basal leaves have long petioles, but the leaf petioles decrease in length as they increase in height on the stem. Although the plants otherwise closely resemble each other, the leaves of golden Alexanders have finely saw-toothed margins, while the leaves of the yellow pimpernel (*Taenidia integerrima*) have smooth margins.

Flower heads have several branches arising from a common point on the stem. Each head usually has 10 to 20 branches, the outer ones perhaps 2 inches long. The tiny individual flowers, usually less than ⅛ inch wide, are a deep yellow-orange color. Close examination shows oblong petals that curve sharply inward at the tips.

Golden Alexanders (*Zizia aurea*) looks like a finely formed, more delicate type of wild parsnip (*Thaspium*). *Zizia* is smaller (2 to 3 feet tall), and the central flower in each umbel flower cluster has no stalk. In *Thaspium,* all flowers and fruits have stalks.

The seeds are flattened ovals about ⅛ inch long and half as wide.

Early European settlers considered the plant to be an anti-syphilitic, a diaphoretic, and a medicine for healing wounds.

The Meskwaki used the root to reduce fever. Flowerstalks were powdered and added to a mixture to produce a snuff whose Meskwaki name translates more or less into "snuff used for illness in the head" — headache.

photograph by Randall A. Maas

Other common names: everlasting, ladies' tobacco, immortelle, plantain-leaved everlasting

Antennaria: from the resemblance of the pappus to the antennae of certain insects

Plantaginifolia: from the shape of the leaves, which resemble those of the plantain

Daisy family: Asteraceae (Compositae)

This low-growing perennial is relegated to the driest prairie sites, often on clay soil or rocky ridges. It is also found on dry, disturbed woodland sites. Flowering occurs from late April to June.

Pussytoes has a rosette of rather large, broad-bladed basal leaves on long stalks. These leaves have three to seven conspicuous veins and resemble the shape of plantain (*Plantago* spp.). The leaves and flowering stem are covered with woolly or silky whitish hairs that give the plant an overall gray appearance.

The flowering stalk, with several narrow leaves and a tight cluster of flower heads, arises from the center of the basal rosette. The rayless flowers are covered with silky hairs, and they are normally unisexual.

Reproduction is more often by leaf-bearing stolons, which allow dense colonies to form, than by seeds.

The Meskwaki used the leaves to prepare a tea that was drunk by the mother each day for 2 weeks after childbirth to prevent her from getting sick. The volatile oils and glucosides of the plant were utilized as a digestive tonic.

Because the dry bracts remain unchanged when the plant is picked for a winter bouquet, it is called everlasting. Although often called ladies' tobacco, no authentic reference for such use can be found.

Because this plant grows on poor soil where little else can, it serves as a valuable soil anchor.

The genus is difficult to separate into species, in part because *Antennaria* has attained the peculiar trait of forming seeds without pollination, which allows it to form many races differing only slightly in physical appearance. While over 30 species of *Antennaria* occur in eastern North America, most are open woodland species. Two species occasionally found on poor soil prairies are *A. neglecta,* with a single vein in the basal leaf, and *A. canescens,* a northern species with bright green basal leaves.

photograph by Sylvan T. Runkel

Other common names: gromwell, hoary puccoon, Indian paint

Lithospermum: from Greek *lethos* for "stone" and *sperma* for "seed"; named for the stonelike seeds

Canescens: from Latin, meaning "generally hoary or whitish," referring to the hoary appearance of the plant due to the presence of tiny white hairs

Forget-me-not family: Boraginaceae

Commonly found in plains and prairies, especially areas tending to be dry, and also in open woods and woodland edges. This species indicates the prairie is in good condition. Blooming period is from April to June.

The leafy, rarely branched stem usually grows 6 to 18 inches tall. Both stem and leaves are covered with a dense, whitish down of soft hairs that gives the plant a gray-green color.

The numerous leaves are small, usually no more than 1½ inches long and less than ½ inch wide, and have no petioles. Leaf edges are without toothing or division. Lower leaves tend to be small, sometimes to the point of resembling scales, and crowd along the stem in an alternate arrangement.

The deep, straight taproot of this perennial is a reddish color. Its juice produces a purple stain.

Individual tubelike flowers without stalks of their own arise from the main flowerstalk. The tube opens into five distinct lobes, forming a flower about ½ inch long and ½ inch across. Bright yellow to deep orange flowers form dense, leafy clusters at the tip of the stem. The individual clusters are flattish and often curled over.

The seeds, approximately ⅛ inch long, are whitish to pale yellow, smooth, and shiny. Four are produced by each flower.

To the Menomini, the white ripened seed of this plant was a type of sacred bead used in special ceremonies. Information on the ceremony and on the exact use of the seed is vague because they hesitated to share this information with European settlers.

Sometimes called Indian paint, *L. canescens* is the most famous of the Indian puccoons (dye plants). A good red dye could be extracted from the larger red roots. *Puccoon* is an American Indian name for a number of plants that produce dyes. European settlers sometimes called it alkanet because of the relationship of *L. canescens* with an Old World plant that yields a dye of that name.

Omaha and Ponca children sometimes chewed the root of *L. canescens* with the gum of *Silphium laciniatum* to give the gum a red color. The flowers were chewed to give gum a yellow color.

Navajos chewed the root of another species, *L. incisum,* for coughs due to colds. They also cooked the roots for food.

Shoshoni women reportedly drank a cold water infusion of stone seed, *L. ruderale,* every day for 6 months to ensure permanent sterility. Laboratory tests have indicated that this plant has some contraceptive effects on rats and rabbits, leading the investigator to propose that the degree of activity of *Lithospermum* plants be measured in P.P.U. (papoose preventative units).

photograph by Tomma Lou Maas

Other common names: crowfoot violet; sometimes birdsfoot violet, but this name is more common for another species, *V. pedata*

Viola: the classical Latin name for this genus

Pedatifida: from Latin, meaning generally "divided from a central point with the divisions also deeply cleft"

Violet family: Violaceae

Found throughout the tallgrass prairie among the grasses of open areas and hillsides where moisture is adequate but not excessive. Large flowers of a rich violet-blue appear from April through June.

Broad leaves with an overall shape resembling that of a fan arise on slender petioles from a short, upright, perennial rhizome. These leaves are divided, usually into three or more parts. Each of these parts is further cleft, almost to the base, into two or four narrow, grasslike lobes. In fact, leaves often appear so grasslike that, prior to flowering, it may be difficult to notice the plant among the prairie grasses. The larger leaves, which may be 4 inches across, are generally slightly hairy along the margins and midribs.

Flowers, which may grow to ¾ inch across, are carried just above the leaves on erect, slender stems that arise from the crown. They have the usual five petals and shape that is typical of violets. The three lowest petals tend to be whitish toward the throat, with a thick fur or beard that is quite noticeable. Inconspicuous flowers without petals may also appear on erect stems that are shorter than the leaf petioles.

This species frequently hybridizes with the birdsfoot violet, *V. pedata*. The birdsfoot violet has smaller flowers and not so deeply cut leaves, and its petals are beardless at the throat.

The fruit of prairie violet is a yellowish gray capsule about ¼ inch long. It contains several small, light brown seeds measuring ¹⁄₁₂ inch long and half as wide. This species and its hybrids with *V. pedata* are easily raised from seed.

Dried whole plants of some violets were used for treating diarrhea. Pliny recommended a garland of violets for headache. Called "Nature's vitamin pill," the leaves of violets have been considered a rich source of vitamin C and, perhaps, of vitamin A.

V. pedata served as a mild laxative, and it was used to induce vomiting. A decoction of its leaves and stems was used for treating pulmonary problems.

Omaha Indian children played games with violets.

Many birds eat the seeds, and wild turkeys relish the tuberous roots of violets.

photograph by John Schwegman

Other common names: comandra, star toadflax

Comandra: from Greek, meaning "hair" and "man," referring to the hairs of the calyx, which are attached to the anthers

Umbellata: like umbels, or umbrella-like flower heads

Sandalwood family: Santalaceae

Found throughout the Upper Midwest in dry ground, prairies, and open woods and also on dry, gravelly or sandy soils. Blooms April into July.

Bastard toadflax grows to a height of over a foot. The alternate leaves are thin and oblong and have a prominent midrib on the underside.

While the many members of the sandalwood family are widely known to be parasitic on the roots of many plants, the roots of *Comandra* are perennial, creeping rhizomes that are only partly parasitic on the roots of other plants, including trees and shrubs. It is doubtful if it ever does serious damage to the host. *Comandra* also has chlorophyll in the leaves and can manufacture its own food.

The small white flowers occur in small clusters at the tips of the flowering stems. The flower has no petals; its five sepals, which appear similar to petals, occur around the rim of a small, funnel-like structure that later becomes the nutlike fruit.

Bastard toadflax spreads by rhizomes and often forms dense stands. Seeds mature in midsummer, after which the plant dies back. Seeds are small, urn-shaped, nutlike fruits that are sweet and oily. Several closely related species have edible fruits.

The fruits were eaten by native Americans. However, the quantity was so small that they were not a major food but rather like a sparse dessert or a trail snack.

Drinking a tea made from the leaves or sucking on immature flowers (as one would a lozenge or cough drop) was considered good for respiratory troubles.

Based on the shapes of the inflorescence and the leaves and the length of the calyx, some authorities recognize three taxa: *C. umbellata, C. pallida,* and *C. richardsiana.* They are wide-ranging in North America, occurring throughout the eastern United States and into the Great Plains.

Although of interest to prairie biologists, *C. umbellata* is of little commercial value. Relatively little is known about the biology of this plant.

photograph by Randall A. Maas

Other common names: none known

Fragaria: from Latin *fraga,* meaning "having scent," probably referring to the fragrance of the fruit

Virginiana: meaning "of Virginia"

Rose family: Rosaceae

Found throughout the tallgrass prairie biome in a variety of habitats, from dry soils of open woodlands and woodland edges to fields and native prairies. It normally grows in colonies. The blooming period is from April to July.

This ground-hugging plant arises from a fibrous, perennial root system. Petioles of leaves are hairy, up to 6 inches long, and arise from tufts on the runners. Each leaf, one per stem, is divided into three leaflets. Leaflets are sharply toothed, broad ovals that are 2 inches in length.

The hairy, erect flowerstalks give rise to sparse, open clusters of white flowers, each of which is usually less than an inch across. The flowers have five individual, rounded petals on a saucer-shaped corolla typical of the rose family. Flowerstalks are shorter than leaf petioles, so the flowers occur below the level of the leaves.

The familiar scarlet wild strawberry develops in June and July. Small "seeds," actually achenes, are imbedded in pits on the surface of the "berry," which really is not a berry but a succulent fruit (receptacle). The fruit is about ½ to ⅔ inch in diameter and has a somewhat irregular globular shape. The flavor of the fruit is sweet, even more delicious than garden varieties. Cultivated strawberries were developed by hybrid crosses from several native stocks.

The less common woodland strawberry, *F. vesca,* is similar but taller. The flowers are as high as the leaves and the achenes protrude from the surface of the fruit.

The wild strawberry was a favorite food of both native Americans and pioneers. It was eaten fresh and was preserved for winter use. Many species of wildlife also eat the berries.

Linnaeus believed that eating wild strawberries cured his gout. Early pioneer medicine utilized the berry for the same reason. However, some people develop an allergic rash from eating wild strawberries.

A tea of dried strawberry leaves was used as an astringent and as a treatment for dysentery and diarrhea. The dried leaves also were used to make a pleasant beverage.

In England, an infusion of strawberry root was once considered a treatment for gonorrhea.

Possibly the widest medicinal use of wild strawberry was as a fruit syrup to provide a pleasant carrier for medicines.

Izaak Walton wrote, "Doubtless God could have made a better berry, but doubtless God never did." Finding a bed of these sweet-tasting berries can be a fringe benefit of a visit to a tallgrass prairie in June or July.

photograph by Sylvan T. Runkel

Other common names: blue camass, eastern camass, Indian potatoes, swamp sego, wild hyacinth

Camassia: from the American Indian name of the plant, *quamash*

Scilloides: from Latin for "like Scilla," an Old World genus of bulbous plants with leaves much like those of this species

Lily family: Liliaceae

This perennial is found on low prairies and open areas of the middle United States where soils are moist to wet in winter and spring but dry in summer. It flowers from April to late May.

A leafless flower stem and the basal leaves of camass grow from a black-coated perennial bulb that is generally 1 to 1½ inches long. The leaves are grasslike—long and narrow—often 12 inches or longer and seldom more than ½ inch across. The center midrib is prominent on the underside. The leaves are mostly green, but in one variety they are variegated with whitish markings.

The top 3 to 8 inches of the flower stem, which is generally less than 2 feet tall, is a loose-flowered cylinder of nearly white to pale blue to purple flowers. This cluster of flowers often contains 10 or more blossoms. Each flower has three petals and three similar sepals that form a six-pointed star ½ to ¾ inch across. The arrangement of the star points may be somewhat uneven. The pale coloring often shows three, sometimes as many as seven, darker veins. Each flower is on a stalk shorter than the width of the flower.

The fruit is a triangular or globular capsule.

There has been some confusion between the western camass (*C. quamash*) and the eastern camass (*C. scilloides*). While much has been recorded about the widespread use of the western species for food, very little seems to have been written about similar uses of the eastern prairie species. Several authorities agree, however, that eastern camass was also used for food by various American Indian tribes.

The edible bulb of the western species was an important food of the Vancouver Indians and probably also of other American Indian tribes. The bulb was boiled, roasted, or cooked with other foods. It was also used to make a sort of molasses. Bulbs of this species were dried for winter use.

A long-lasting fire was made by layering bulbs, pine needles, and soil together.

C. scilloides has been used for ornamental purposes. Its seeds will grow in slightly acid soil.

The poisonous death camas (*Zigadenus* sp.) has sometimes been confused with *Camassia*—with unfortunate results. *Zigadenus,* however, is an entirely different genus.

photograph by John Schwegman

Other common names: American sanicle, rock geranium, ground maple, cliffweed

Heuchera: in honor of Johann Heinrich von Heucher, an early German physician and botanist who specialized in medicinal botany

Richardsonii: in honor of Sir John Richardson, an early North American explorer. (Several varieties of this species occur.)

Saxifrage family: Saxifragaceae

Found throughout the prairie biome, mostly on drier or sandy sites on the prairie. It flowers from April to June.

The basal leaves, shaped somewhat like those of the hard maple, are supported by long petioles that arise from a perennial crown. The leaves, 2 to 3 inches across, have rounded, shallow lobes and coarsely toothed margins. Veins on the undersides of the leaves are lined with tiny white hairs. The petioles and the flowering stalk are covered with long white hairs. When present, leaves along the flowering stem are alternate and widely spaced.

The fibrous rootstock is black and coarse and has many branching rootlets.

The flowering stalk is normally leafless. It grows from 1 to 2 feet tall and stands well above the basal leaves. The flowering spike is large, equaling as much as one-third of the height of the plant, but the infloresence is relatively inconspicuous.

The flowers are somewhat bell-shaped and droop on individual short stalks that branch from the main flowerstalk. The small flowers, only ¼ inch long, have five spatula-shaped petals that vary from white to pale green to lavender; the upper petals are slightly longer than the lower ones. Stamens are tipped with brilliant orange anthers and extend beyond the petals. The five green sepals, nearly as large as the petals, are often unequal in size.

The fruit is a dry, single-celled, oval capsule containing several tiny seeds.

Native Americans and early pioneers used a powder made from the roots of this plant as an astringent to close wounds. This powder also served as a treatment for diarrhea and for a sore throat. The Meskwaki used the green leaves to prepare an astringent dressing for open sores.

The common name alumroot is derived from the puckering alumlike taste imparted by the root. Another common wildflower, wild geranium, is sometimes also called alumroot because of similar properties.

A more eastern species, *H. americana,* has yellowish green, drooping flowers on a hairy stalk; the flowers are in a loose, branching cluster. While several other species occur in the Upper Midwest, *H. richardsonii* and *H. americana* are the only ones that appear on the tallgrass prairie.

A common cultivated garden flower, coralbells, is perhaps the best-known member of this genus. It is very similar in appearance but with flowers that range from pink to deep crimson.

photograph by John Schwegman

Kittentails: *Besseya bullii* (Eat.) Rydb., also called *Wulfenia bullii* (Eat.) Barnh.

29

Other common names: Bull's synthyris

Besseya: named for Bessey, a well-known botanist

Bullii: named for its discoverer, George Bull

Snapdragon family: Scrophulariaceae

Found on dry prairies, bluffs, and oak barrens from southern Michigan to Minnesota, south to Ohio, Indiana, Illinois, and Iowa, but its range in each state is limited to a few locations. Blooms May and early June.

This perennial herb grows from a thickened rootstock. The stem, which may get nearly a foot high, is covered with short hairs.

The leaves are mostly basal, and they usually lie flat on the ground. These thick, basal leaves are ovate, rounded at the top, cordate at the base, and toothed. Stem leaves are reduced and alternate.

The greenish yellow corolla, which is less than ¼ inch in length, has an entire upper lip and a usually irregularly lobed, three-part lower lip. Flowers are clustered in a dense terminal spike.

No medicinal or food uses of this plant by pioneers or American Indians are known. However, because of its unique appearance, it is certain that it did not go unnoticed.

Kittentails is a rare midwestern endemic that is encountered most often in the driest parts of a prairie; it often occurs in large colonies. (The little kittentails and pussytoes like to keep their feet dry, while the big cattail prefers to go wading in the wetter parts of the prairie.)

Many flower enthusiasts have not seen it, partly due to its early blooming habit and partly due to its scarcity. Wildflower gardeners who like to grow unusual plants would do well to attempt growing this one!

Another species of kittentails, *B. wyomingensis,* is generally found farther west in the hills and mountains of South Dakota, Nebraska, Colorado, Utah, and Idaho.

photograph by William P. Pusateri

Other common names: old man's whiskers, Johnny smokers

Geum: the ancient Latin name used by Pliny for this group

Triflorum: from Latin, meaning "three-flowered"

Rose family: Rosaceae

Found in Midwest prairies and to the north and east, including New York, the shores of Lake Huron, and from Ontario to Alberta. Among the earliest to appear, prairie smoke usually begins flowering in April or May and continues through June.

Flowering stems and numerous basal leaves arise from a perennial rootstock. The leaves have petioles and are compound, with 7 to 15 leaflets arranged along a midrib 4 to 9 inches long. Each leaflet is deeply cut, so the total effect is somewhat fernlike. The two or three clefts in the end leaflet are not so deep, less than half the leaflet length. Stem leaves are few, small, and opposite. Both the stem and the leaves have a covering of soft hairs.

Flowering stems are 6 to 16 inches tall. The stems branch into three, sometimes as many as eight, flowerstalks at the top. About halfway up each flowerstalk is a pair of small leaflets.

Five oval petals stand mostly erect to form a cup about ¾ inch across. The petals vary from reddish brown to pinkish to yellowish and sometimes a flesh color. At the base of the flower are five green sepals. Narrow, linear bracts alternate with the sepals.

The fruits have plumelike gray tails about 2 inches long. As a result, the heads resemble minute feather dusters when the plants occur close together in colonies. Fruits of most species of *Geum* are a characteristic hooked sticktight that clings tightly to clothing or animal fur.

Roots of prairie smoke (*G. triflorum*) were used to make a beverage resembling weak sassafras tea. Early settlers drank the tea for colic, for most ailments of the digestive tract, and for uterine hemorrhage. It also served as a fever reducer, a powerful astringent, and a styptic.

American Indians made a tea of the roots. An eastern species, *G. virginianum,* also was used to make a medicinal tea.

The Blackfoot made a decoction of the roots for an eyewash. The Ojibwa boiled roots of *G. strictum* for a weak decoction that was taken internally for soreness in the chest and for a cough.

The Chippewa used *G. canadense* for "diseases of women." *G. rivale* was used as a gargle for a sore throat.

Called Indian chocolate, *G. rivale* is found in wet or marshy areas. It was one of the early "sugar-coated" medicines. It contained a tannin used as a powerful astringent, and it was widely used for dysentery. A root decoction was mixed with sugar and milk to make a beverage substitute for cocoa.

photograph by Tomma Lou Maas

Biscuitroot: *Lomatium foeniculaceum* (Nutt.) C. & R.

Other common names: wild parsley, hairy parsley, lomatium, carrot-leaf lomatium, Indian biscuit, cowas or cows

Lomatium: from the Greek, meaning "a little border," referring to the winged borders on the fruit

Foeniculaceum: meaning "like fennel"

Parsley family: Apiaceae (Umbelliferae)

Generally found in the central and western part of the tall-grass prairie from Canada to Missouri and Texas, it usually occurs on drier portions of the prairie. The biscuitroots are early spring blooming plants. By June most of them are in fruit. Blooms April to June.

The parsley-like leaves, divided into three main parts, are lower than the fruiting stem (peduncle), which may be 8 to 10 inches tall. It has a relatively large, long root that helps it to exist in drier soils. The root is edible.

The five-petaled yellow flowers are in umbels. Some other species of biscuitroot have white or purplish flowers.

The flattened, winged fruits are ¼ to ⅜ inch long; they are rounded to elliptic in shape and have very noticeable dorsal ribs. The fruits are edible.

Biscuitroot has a tie-in with our country's history: it was one of the native plant foods that the Lewis and Clark expedition secured through trade with American Indians. One excerpt from Lewis and Clark's recorded notes says, "On the second day of June, 1806, two men were sent out to trade with the Indians [in Idaho]. They returned with three bushels of edible roots and some cowas bread" (made of the same material). These edible roots were one of the many species of lomatium—all of which apparently have edible roots.

Some authorities say there are about 60 species of lomatium. Many are found in the northwestern part of the United States and in the Great Plains. There are at least two species that come as far east as Nebraska and Iowa; both have been found in the Loess Hills of western Iowa.

Biscuitroots, as they are called collectively, were one of the most important articles of trade among American Indians. When eaten raw, the roots were said to taste like celery. Usually the roots were peeled, dried, and ground into a kind of flour, which was then shaped into cakes. European settlers said these cakes had the taste of stale biscuits, hence, the name biscuitroot. When food for long trips was needed, these cakes were sometimes made large enough to be strapped to the saddle.

Earlier, the lomatiums were given the genus name *Peucedanum,* the name of a European plant. However, the European plant was much taller, grew in wet locations, and differed in other ways. Now the lomatiums have their own genus name. They are sometimes planted as border plants and do well in dry, exposed situations.

L. orientale, with bipinnate leaves and white to pink flowers, occurs in the dry parts of the Great Plains.

photograph by Sylvan T. Runkel

Other common names: downy phlox

Phlox: from Greek for "flame," an ancient name for *Lychnis* that was later transferred to this genus

Pilosa: from Latin, meaning "softly hairy"

Phlox family: Polemoniaceae

Found throughout the tallgrass prairie and in dry, open woods and other cleared areas. Flowering time is April to June.

Leafy stems grow 8 to 30 inches tall from a perennial taproot. The stems are hairy, seldom branched, and mostly erect. Stems bearing flowers tend to be less leafy than the others. A second species, *P. maculata,* has stems that are not hairy and are conspicuously spotted with purple.

The leaves are 1 to 4 inches long and less than ⅓ inch across. They are somewhat rounded toward the base but narrow to a stiff, sharp tip. Leaves grow opposite each other and have no petiole (leaf stem). The upper leaves may tend to clasp the stem.

The flower head is a group of loosely branched clusters. Each cluster has a few flowers, each on its own short stalk. The individual flower, perhaps ¾ inch across, is a five-ribbed tube flaring to five rounded lobes. The lobes are wider toward the tip than toward the base. The color varies from pink to rose to violet. *P. maculata* has a wider range of color: purple to red-violet to whitish.

Bracts, the modified leaves at the base of each flower, are conspicuously pointed and awned.

The fruit is a small, oval capsule with two or three cells, each containing a single seed. The seed capsule tends to "explode" when mature and dry.

The Meskwaki made a tea of the leaves and used it as a wash for treating eczema. The same sort of tea was drunk to cure eczema and to purify the blood at the same time. Also, the root was used with several other unspecified plants as part of a love potion.

The prairie phlox is often visited by hummingbirds, and it is occasionally eaten by deer. *P. hoodii* (moss phlox), found in dry western areas, has spiny leaves, so sheep graze only on the flowers.

Many of the phlox species have a sticky substance on their upper stems to protect them against insects that do not serve as carriers of pollen.

Several garden varieties have been adapted from these native species.

photograph by Sylvan T. Runkel

Other common names: small pussy willow, upland willow, low willow, bush willow

Salix: the classical Latin name for this widespread genus

Humilis: from Latin, meaning "low," in reference to the low-growing habit of this species. (This species frequently hybridizes with several others of the genus, especially the pussy willow, *S. discolor.*)

Willow family: Salicaceae

Found in dry prairies and open spaces throughout the area east of the Great Plains. Flowers April through May.

This shrubby perennial is highly variable, growing from 1 foot to nearly 10 feet tall. The smooth bark of the wandlike branches is a dull yellowish to brownish color.

The alternate leaves are oval to lance-shaped, tapering gently at both ends. They are a dark grayish green above. The underside is lighter colored, strongly veined, and sometimes covered with fine hairs. Margins may be smooth or sparingly toothed.

The leaves are usually 2 to 4 inches long and about ½ inch wide. Leaves near the middle of the plant are broader than those higher or lower on the plant. The leaves are on petioles less than ½ inch long. There is a small, leaf-shaped appendage (stipule) where the leaf petiole joins the stem.

In April or May, long before the leaves appear, the wandlike flowering branches are covered with flowering spikes called catkins. These fluffy catkins are dense ovals adjacent to the stem. The larger, darker-colored ones, sometimes more than 1 inch long, are female. The shorter, smaller, male-flowered catkins are often tinged with the red or purple color of the unopened anthers (male flower parts that produce pollen).

Seeds are minute and have a tuft of long white hairs that allow them to be widely distributed by wind.

Most willows have been used since the time of Christ for their pain-relieving and fever-reducing qualities. Early settlers used the bark to make a bitter tonic, an astringent, and a treatment for intermittent fever. Fresh bark contains salicin, which probably decomposes to salicylic acid in the human body. (Aspirin gets its effect from a chemically related salicylic acid.)

The Menomini used the roots as a spasmodic and for colic and diarrhea. The Potawatomi boiled root bark of *S. discolor* for a tea to stop bleeding, and the Meskwaki used the roots to prepare a tea as an enema for flux. The leaves have been used as a poultice to stop bleeding and to treat colic. Some American Indian tribes considered the catkins of a related species, black willow (*S. nigra*), to be an aphrodisiac.

Buds and small twigs are a staple food of grouse and, farther north, of ptarmigans. Rabbits, elk, moose, and deer eat twigs, foliage, and bark.

The pliable twigs of this and other willows have been used for making baskets.

photograph by Sylvan T. Runkel

Other common names: American vetch, purple vetch, stiffleaf vetch

Vicia: classical Latin name for this genus

Americana: meaning "of America"

Legume family: Fabaceae (Leguminosae)

Found in prairies and plains, especially on moist soils. Two varieties of vetch occur westward and are separated on the basis of leaf-width. Vetch is widely distributed, but it is not normally found in dense colonies. Blooms May to August.

The smooth stems of this vetch are slender and weak. They grow to 3 feet long and tend to trail or climb. The compound leaves have four to nine pairs of opposite leaflets. The terminal "leaf" is a tendril. Individual leaflets are elliptic in shape and have smooth margins. Leaflets are usually ⅗ to 1⅓ inches long and up to ½ inch wide.

Bluish purple, pea-like flowers are borne in loose clusters that arise from axils of the upper leaves. The clusters of three to nine flowers are shorter than the adjacent leaves. The individual flowers, like those of the pea, have two lips or lobes. The upper lip is shorter than the lower one.

Tender seeds and young stems were eaten by native Americans and European settlers. People have eaten the green seeds of some species like peas. Since some species are poisonous, it is important that a vetch be correctly identified before using it for any purpose—or serious consequences may result.

Some vetches have been planted to improve soils and to furnish hay and pasture. The plants provide excellent forage and are often overgrazed because of livestock preference. They are also grazed by deer, and game birds use them for food.

There are about two dozen species of *Vicia* in the United States. *V. americana* is a native species, but many of the vetches that have been planted are from Europe or the Old World. (The legume is sometimes called tare in England, a name that found its way into the New Testament.) The common hairy vetch, *V. villosa,* although not native, is commonly planted and seen along roadsides all across the country.

photograph by Ted Van Bruggen

Other common names: roosterheads, American cowslip, bird-bills, Indian chief, pride-of-Ohio, Johnny jump

Dodecatheon: from Greek for "twelve gods," a name originally applied to another plant and later transferred to this genus

Meadia: in honor of Dr. Richard Mead, an early English physician and botanist

Primrose family: Primulaceae

Found throughout the eastern portion of the tallgrass prairie biome, west to central Iowa, on mesic to dry sites or rocky, dry, wooded ridges. Flowering occurs from late April to June.

In early spring, a basal rosette of leaves of this species arises from a short, perennial rootstock. These leaves, which have reddish bases and midribs, are spatula-shaped and may be up to 8 inches long. The leaves become narrow toward the base, often to the extent of having a winged petiole. Leaf margins are generally smooth and wavy, but occasionally they have shallow, rounded teeth.

The smooth, hollow, leafless flowerstalk arises from the center of the rosette of leaves and achieves a height of from 6 to 20 inches. At the top, it divides into numerous arching branches, each terminating in an individual flower.

Flowers number from a few to 20 or more. The individual flowers may be up to an inch across. The attractive flowers, which range from white to a deep lilac, each have five narrow petals that are joined at their bases by a short tube. The petals diverge upward, away from the base, to form a starlike pattern. A beaklike cone composed of stamens protrudes from the center, accentuating its shooting-star shape. Pollination is achieved by bumblebees.

During flowering, the peduncle is curved so that the flowers point downward. As the seeds develop and the flowers wither after pollination, the peduncle straightens until the small, barrel-shaped capsule stands erect, a position that allows better dispersal of the seeds.

Despite its beauty, or perhaps because of it, few medicinal uses can be found. It may have been used as an "emergency" food by native Americans.

A second species, the jeweled shooting star (*D. amethystinum*), occurs in the tallgrass prairie biome but prefers damp, thin, limestone soil sites on the bluffs of the Mississippi River. It is smaller and has rose-crimson flowers.

There seems to be little agreement on the classification of this genus. Some authorities feel there are over 30 species, others feel there are only a few. This discrepancy may result from the unusually high ecological tolerance of the species.

photograph by Sylvan T. Runkel

Other common names: meadow garlic, wild onion, wild shallot

Allium: ancient Latin name for garlic

Canadense: meaning "of Canada"

Lily family: Liliaceae

Found throughout the tallgrass prairie and in open woods and thickets. Blooms May to July.

A strong, onionlike odor is characteristic of this entire genus. The narrow, linear, leaves are up to 1½ feet long. They are flattened on one surface, slightly convex on the other. Unlike some *Allium* species, the leaves of wild garlic are not hollow.

The grass-like leaves arise from a shallow bulb that seldom measures more than 1 inch thick. Its outer coat is brown and fibrous; the inner leaves are white and shiny. The bulb may subdivide as one means of reproduction.

A flowerstalk as tall as 2 feet also rises from the bulb. It is topped with a spherical cluster of numerous aerial bulblets. These little whitish to purple bulblets drop to the ground and take root. Sometimes the bulblets have long slender "tails." The cluster may also have a few flowers extending from it on individual stalks.

The slender flowers have six white to pinkish petals. The petals and colored sepals are usually separated at their bases. Two or three rather broad bracts enclose the base of the flower.

The fruit is a small capsule containing one or two black seeds in each of three segments.

The antiseptic properties of wild garlic, one of the most powerful herbs, were known to American Indians and pioneers. Plant juices were often applied to wounds and burns. The Cheyenne crushed bulbs and stems to form a poultice for boils. The Dakota and the Winnebago found such a poultice provided relief from bee stings, and some tribes used it for snakebite. Early pioneers commonly used wild garlic as a substitute for an onion poultice.

American Indians and pioneers sliced the bulbs, cooked them, and dissolved maple sugar in the liquid to form a cough syrup. This mixture was also considered a good treatment for hives. Other pioneer medicinal uses of wild garlic were for the treatment of fevers, disorders of the blood, lung troubles, internal parasites, skin problems, hemorrhoids, earache, rheumatism, and arthritis.

Early explorers used wild garlic to control scurvy. When Father Marquette made his famous journey from Green Bay to the present site of Chicago, wild garlic was an important part of the food supply.

Some ancient civilizations credited wild garlic and other relatives of the onion with divine properties that could impart strength and courage, foster love, and remove jealousy.

There are at least 10 species of *Allium* in North America, and none are poisonous. However, species of *Zigadenus*, sometimes called death camas, have been mistaken for wild onion. *Zigadenus,* however, does not have an onionlike odor.

photograph by Ted Van Bruggen

Other common names: buffalo apple, buffalo pea, buffalo plum, milk vetch

Astragalus: ancient Greek name for a leguminous plant. It actually means "star" and "milk." (This is one of the largest genera of flowering plants in North America.)

Crassicarpus: from Latin and Greek, meaning "thick pod," which aptly describes the thick, rounded fruit pods of this species

Legume family: Fabaceae (Leguminosae)

Found throughout the tallgrass prairie and west on dry upland soils. Blooms May and June.

The short, hairy stems of ground plum, usually less than 15 inches long, tend to sprawl along the ground with the tips ascending. The perennial rootstock branches profusely and sends up new stems along its length.

The alternate leaves are typical of the vetches; they have a series of small leaflets paired opposite along the central stem and one at the tip. These medium green leaflets are slender ovals up to ½ inch long and about ⅛ inch wide. Leaflets have smooth margins. The underside is covered with tiny, stiff hairs.

In May and June as many as 10 large flowers, perhaps an inch long, are borne along a central flowerstalk at the end of the stem or on flowerstalks arising from upper leaf axils. These flowerstalks are generally shorter than the leaves. Petal color ranges from pale purple to white, often with markings of deeper purple. The keel, the lowest petal of the pea-like flower, is short

and rounded. This is unlike the closely related *Oxytropis* genus (crazyweeds) in which the keel is long and pointed. Otherwise, identification may be difficult even for botanists.

Unripe fruits, about ½ inch in diameter, are smooth and succulent and resemble plums. As they approach maturity, the upper side (which is exposed to the sun) becomes purple, while the protected underside remains green. As the fruit dries, it becomes "corky" with a tough, thick skin. Thus protected, fruits often persist into following years. Each fruit contains numerous black seeds.

Some American Indians chewed small amounts of ground plum leaves for a sore throat. They used a decoction of boiled root for toothache and as an external application for insect bites.

The Chippewa treated convulsions with the dried and powdered root, and the root was used in combination with other plants for controlling bleeding from wounds. This species also provided an ingredient of Chippewa war medicine.

Before the fruits dry, they closely resemble small, green plums. They were an important food of American Indians and early settlers, who ate them either raw or cooked. The fruit was sometimes made into spiced pickles. (Fruits of some other species of the genus are poisonous.)

The Omaha and the Ponca gathered the fruits at corn-planting time, soaked them with the corn seed, threw away the fruits, and planted the corn. This is an old custom, the origin of which has been forgotten.

photograph by Ted Van Bruggen

Other common names: long-bracted wild indigo, plains wild indigo, large-bracted wild indigo, yellowish false indigo

Baptisia: from the Greek *baptizein,* "to dye," referring to the economic use of some species that yield a poor indigo dye

Leucophaea: meaning "cream-colored"

Legume family: Fabaceae (Leguminosae)

Found on prairies throughout the tallgrass biome, similar to the range of *B. leucantha,* prairie false indigo. Blooms May to June.

Cream-colored false indigo is a coarse, hairy plant with spreading branches. It may achieve a height of 3 feet but is normally closer to 1 foot tall.

The leaf stipules of this plant are so large that they appear to be leaflets, which makes the leaf appear to have five leaflets instead of the three of *B. leucantha.*

The yellowish or cream-colored flowers tend to be reclining, recumbent, or drooping. The flower spike may reach a foot in length.

The pods, which are ovoid and narrowed at the base, end in a sort of beak and are 1 to 2 inches long. Numerous seeds are contained in the pods.

In the dormant stage, the plant is commonly found separated from the root system. In this stage it still has leaves and pods attached, and it is tumbled by the wind. This characteristic aids in seed dispersal.

This plant was used medicinally by American Indians to treat cuts and certain fevers. The Pawnee pulverized the seeds and mixed the powder with buffalo fat; this ointment was rubbed on the abdomen as a treatment for colic.

Indian boys often used seedpods as rattles when they imitated their elders at a ceremonial dance.

Although this species is distasteful to livestock, it is occasionally found persisting in grazed pastures where bluegrass has replaced the native species. It and related species have been responsible for poisoning livestock, especially horses.

This species has been cultivated, and it occasionally escapes.

B. tinctoria, with yellow flowers and many racemes, is a northeastern species that occasionally is found on prairie remnants. *B. australis,* with bluish purple flowers, is a southern plant of glades and dry prairies.

The early blooming habit of *B. leucophaea* adds color to the early, otherwise drab, spring prairie landscape.

photograph by LeRoy G. Pratt

Other common names: prairie shoestring, wild tea

Amorpha: from the Greek *amorphos,* meaning generally "without shape" or "deformed," in reference to the flower, which has only one petal

Canescens: from Latin, meaning "gray hairy"

Legume family: Fabaceae (Leguminosae)

Found on dry, sandy soils throughout the tallgrass prairie, often in dense colonies. Also found in rocky, open woodlands. Blooming time is late May to August.

As a shrubby perennial, often as an undershrub in big bluestem, lead plant grows to 3 feet tall. The stems may become woody with age and be as much as ½ inch in diameter.

The numerous compound leaves occur opposite along the stems. Each leaf has numerous pairs of small, oval leaflets arranged in pairs opposite, plus one leaflet at the tip. Leaves, 2 to 4 inches long, may have as many as 25 pairs of leaflets. An individual leaflet may be as much as ½ inch long and ¼ inch wide.

The entire plant is hairy, so much so that it has a whitish appearance; this whitish cast lends a lead color to dense patches, hence, its common name.

Lead plant is deep-rooted, so it draws its moisture from soil below that which serves most prairie plants.

Tiny purple flowers are in a spikelike mass along the upper 2 to 7 inches of the stems. Each flower has a single petal (the standard of a typical legume or pea flower) but no wings or keel.

Protruding yellow stamens are conspicuous parts of the flowers.

Fruits are dotted, fuzzy pods; each contains a single, brown, bean-shaped seed. Pods are about ¼ inch long. The total seed head has a distinctive purple-gray color.

The Oglala and other American Indians used dried leaves for smoking and for making tea. Lead plant was made into tea as treatment for pinworms. Leaves were steeped and the liquid was used as a wash to treat eczema. The Omaha used it to prepare a moxa for rheumatism and neuralgia.

Some *Amorpha* species have been used as dyes.

The Omaha and the Ponca called it *te-hu to-hi,* meaning "buffalo bellow plant," probably because it flowers in the bison rutting season. It also is an important food for browsing animals.

Lead plant is often cultivated as an ornamental.

Its presence is an indicator of a prairie in good condition. Local superstitions held that the lead plant was an indication of the presence of lead ore.

There are about 15 American species of *Amorpha.*

photograph by Richard F. Trump

Other common names: large white wild indigo, Atlantic wild indigo, white false indigo

Baptisia: from the Greek, meaning "to dye," referring to the use of some species as a poor-quality indigo dye

Leucantha: meaning "white-flowered"

Legume family: Fabaceae (Leguminosae)

Found throughout the tallgrass prairie on rich, sometimes wet, prairie soils. Blooms May to June.

This 2- to 5-foot high, stout, upright, gray-green perennial has smooth stems and succulent, ascending branches. The leaves are alternate and have small, sharp stipules. There are three leaflets per leaf. Each leaflet, 1 to 2 inches long and ½ to 1 inch wide, is widely rounded at the end and narrow at the base. The leaves turn black on drying.

The 1-inch long white flowers occur on a terminal, upright raceme (open spike) that may be up to 1 foot or more long. The flowers are similar to pea flowers.

The blackish pods, which tend to droop, are about ¾ inch long. They are connected to the calyx by a relatively long stalk.

In the early stages of growth, prairie false indigo resembles asparagus, but it is poisonous and should not be eaten. The entire plant, green or dried in hay, is poisonous to horses and cattle.

B. leucantha, which contains alkaloids, was included in early lists of medicinal plants. Boiled roots were used to treat chronic colds. Some early settlers made a decoction of the root to treat scarlet fever, typhus, and epidemic dysentery.

It served as an emetic, a cathartic, and a coloring agent. *B. tinctoria* was probably also used.

The Meskwaki used prairie false indigo as a cure for sores that were slow to heal, as an emetic, and as a treatment for eczema. It was combined with sycamore bark as a medicine for axe or knife wounds and combined with senega snakeroot (*Polygala senega*) for snakebite.

Some Plains Indians used a decoction of the leaves as a stimulant; they also applied it to cuts and wounds.

This species was regarded by some beekeepers as a source of a light amber honey with a characteristic flavor. Children once used its dry pods as toy rattles. In colonial times it served as a dye, but it was less satisfactory than true indigo.

Another species, *B. tinctoria,* is called horsefly weed because of the custom of tying a bunch of it to a horse's harness to repel flies.

photograph by John Schwegman

Other common names: breadroot, pomme blanche, pomme de prairie, prairie potato, tipsin, tipsinna

Psoralea: from Greek, meaning "scurfy" or "scabby," from the glandular spots on the leaves, stem, and calyx

Esculenta: from Latin *esculentus,* meaning "fit for food"

Legume family: Fabaceae (Leguminosae)

Found on dry prairies and calcareous hills from Iowa to the northern and western Great Plains. Blooming period is from May to July.

The prairie turnip, an erect perennial that is usually less than a foot tall, is densely covered with whitish hairs. The alternate and palmately compound leaves are generally divided into five leaflets. The leaflets are 1 to 2 inches long and usually ½ inch or less wide; they have smooth margins. The petioles are two to four times longer than the leaves.

Flowers are arranged in dense spikes that are 1½ to 3 inches long and up to 1½ inches thick. Bracts are ⅔ inch long, nearly equaling the bluish corolla. The small, pea-like flowers are deep blue to purple and only ⅛ inch across and ¾ inch long.

The oblong pod is up to 2½ inches long and contains a single seed.

An abscission layer at ground level allows the plant to become free soon after the seeds have ripened and to tumble across the prairie, scattering seeds. Late in the season this species is apparent only as dead plants scattered on the prairie.

Several inches below the surface of the ground, the root forms an enlargement, or turnip, the size of a hen's egg. These roots were dug by native Americans in June and July. This harvest had to occur after the tops had dried down but before the plants were blown loose. Gathering these from the hard prairie soil was no easy task, but the prairie turnip was an important item in the diet of the Plains Indians. The roots were peeled and eaten raw or were cooked by boiling or roasting. Peeled roots were braided into long strings (as is still done with garlic) and hung out to dry. The dried roots, a winter food supply, were often pounded into a starchy meal.

Related species were of value for medicinal purposes. *P. argophylla* has seeds that were reported to have poisoned a child. This plant was used medicinally to treat wounds. Its roots were a mild stimulant, and the Meskwaki used the root tea for chronic constipation. The Cheyenne made a tea of its leaves to lower fever. It was the European settler's remedy for snakebite. The root of *P. tenuiflora* was boiled with other plants and used by the Teton Dakota to treat consumption.

Lewis and Clark recorded buying "bread root" frequently from American Indians, and it is reported that the early pioneers often bought prairie turnips. Although the prairie turnip was common on the prairie, the prairie flora was largely unknown to the pioneers traveling west in prairie schooners. They drove over the same kinds of food plants that they were buying from the Plains Indians.

photograph by Tomma Lou Maas

Other common names: round-leaved anemone, crowfoot

Anemone: from a Greek term meaning "wind," probably referring to the distribution of seeds by the wind or perhaps because the delicate leaves and stems sometimes tremble in the wind. Some authorities believe the origin goes back to a Semitic word for the mythological Adonis.

Canadensis: meaning "of Canada"

Buttercup family: Ranunculaceae

Found commonly throughout eastern North America, Canada anemone occurs in the more moist parts of prairies in calcareous or alluvial soils, along railroads, and even in moist roadside ditches. It does not compete well with the taller members of the prairie flora, but it thrives in wet, disturbed soils at pothole edges. Blooming in late May and lasting through early July, its flowering is one of the early events on prairies.

The plant grows to a height of 2 feet, but it usually is shorter. The leaves are deeply five- to seven-parted and have hairy, prominent veins. The basal leaves have long petioles and are found in whorls of three; the upper leaves are paired.

The solitary, showy white flower, up to 1½ inches across, lacks true petals, but petal-like sepals give this hardy perennial a handsome appearance. The flower is on a long stalk. This stalk holds the flower aloft for pollination by bees and flies and elevates the seed head, aiding the distribution of the seeds by the wind.

The seed head is globular and composed of flat achenes. Reproduction is more commonly by the spread of slender, tough rhizomes than by seed.

The Meskwaki made a tea of anemone roots to treat headache and dizziness—and even to refocus crossed eyes, although for this it seems to have been of more psychological than physical value.

An ancient legend tells that an anemone sprang up where each teardrop of the mythological Venus struck the earth as she mourned the death of her beloved Adonis.

This coarse, hardy perennial sometimes exists in large colonies. It is of little economic importance, but since it has considerable aesthetic value, it is frequently grown in wildflower gardens.

Other tall *Anemone* species grace the prairie landscape. A thimbleweed, the long-fruited anemone (*A. cylindrica*), has a woolly, elongate head with a five- to nine-parted bract below the flower. Another thimbleweed, *A. virginiana,* is very similar but differs by having a two- to three-parted bract below the flower head.

photograph by LeRoy G. Pratt

Other common names: mountain snow, variegated spurge, white-margined spurge, wolf's milk, milkweed (incorrect)

Euphorbia: named in honor of Euphorbus, who was a physician to King Juba of Numidia

Marginata: alluding to the broad white margins of the leaves, especially the upper leaves of the plant

Spurge family: Euphorbiaceae

Originally found in open lands and prairies from Minnesota and Iowa west to Colorado and south to Texas, it has been planted as an ornamental east to the coast, where it has escaped from cultivation and is often found growing in disturbed and waste areas. Many people consider it a weed. Blooms May through October.

The stout, erect stems of snow-on-the-mountain grow to 3 feet tall, although they are usually shorter. Since each stem has a tendency to fork into two stems and each of these forks again, the result is a rather compact, densely branched upper part of the plant.

The alternate leaves are oval and 1 to 3½ inches long. The leaves secrete a milky, acrid juice that is irritating to the skin and is poisonous if ingested. The upper leaves, which are just below and adjacent to the small, rather inconspicuous flowers, are edged in a band of white. From a distance, this band looks like snow, hence, the common name snow-on-the-mountain. This white border is a unique and easily identifiable characteristic of the species.

The tiny white flowers are grouped together in the middle of a flat cluster of white or white-margined leaves or bracts. The flowers, each with a green, roundish, three-sectioned ovary, have a typical spurge appearance.

The Dakota gave mothers without milk a tea made from the plant (the milky sap is poisonous, so the use of this was risky). They also crushed the leaves in warm water and applied this mixture to swellings.

It is reported that the juices of this plant have served as a substitute for the branding iron used in branding cattle. Livestock normally will not eat this plant because of its bitter taste, but they sometimes eat it in dry hay and may be poisoned by it.

Honey made from the flowers of this plant is reported to be bad tasting and poisonous.

Despite its poisonous nature, the plant has been and still is planted widely because of its beauty. The plant is an annual that can be easily controlled if it becomes a problem. Since snow-on-the-mountain is unusually free from fungus and from insect pests, the plants generally are healthy.

It is a close relative of one of our most popular Christmas plants, the poinsettia.

photograph by Ted Van Bruggen

Other common names: star-grass

Hypoxis: an ancient Greek name for some plant with sour leaves, later transferred to this genus by Linnaeus. The Latin meaning of *hypoxis* is "somewhat acid."

Hirsuta: from Latin, meaning generally "covered with stiff hairs"

Daffodil family: Amaryllidaceae

Found in dry prairies and open woods throughout the area east of the Great Plains. It may also be found in wetter areas, especially where the lime content is high. Blooms May through June.

This small, grasslike plant is a perennial. It grows from a small, hard, hairy corm that is ¼ to ½ inch in diameter. The corm is elliptic in shape, has numerous fibrous roots, and varies from pale to dark brown in color.

The hairy, grasslike leaves originate from the base of the plant. They generally are 4 to 12 inches long.

The star-shaped yellow flowers are about ¾ inch across and have three petals and three similar sepals. When the flower is upright and almost closed, it appears green because the outside of the petals is displayed; when the flower is open, it appears golden yellow because the inner side of the petals is displayed. Petals and sepals may be ¼ to ½ inch long and perhaps ⅛ inch wide. There is a rather prominent stamen at the base of each petal and sepal.

The slender, threadlike flowering stems may be erect to re-clining and are 2 to 12 inches long. They carry the flowers below the top of the leaves. Stems may carry two to seven flowers, but only one or two are open at one time during the flowering season.

The fruit is a small, three-celled, oval-shaped capsule containing several small, shiny, black seeds. These tiny seeds, perhaps ⅟₁₆ inch in diameter, are rough, with short, hard points that are prominent under magnification.

Preparations of the root (corm) have long been used to treat ulcers. However, most members of the Amaryllidaceae are known to be poisonous when taken internally.

Yellow star-grass is a relative of the showy amaryllis and the greenhouse bulb plant, *H. stellata,* which bears a larger white flower that is green striped on the outside.

photograph by Randall A. Maas

Other common names: wild iris, fleur-de-lis

Iris: from Greek, meaning "rainbow," probably because of the multitude of flower colors in this genus. Iris was the name of the rainbow goddess of Greek mythology.

Virginica: meaning "of Virginia." *Shrevei,* the variety name, honors Ralph Shreve, botanist.

Iris family: Iridaceae

Found throughout the tallgrass biome, mainly on saturated soils at the edges of marshes and prairie potholes. Blooms May through July.

The narrow, sword-shaped leaves, normally about an inch wide, may grow to 3 feet in length. They have a gray-green cast and grow erect but with a slight, graceful curve. The parallel-veined leaves clasp the flowerstalk at the base. The flowering stalk, which is round in cross section (terete), is occasionally branched, with each branch ending in a showy inflorescence.

The perennial rootstock consists of a fleshy, horizontal rhizome with many fibrous roots. Leaf scars from previous growth show on the rhizome.

Though it is smaller and simpler and has narrower petals, the blue-violet flower resembles that of the cultivated iris. An individual plant usually has multiple flowers, but since normally only one flower is blooming at any time, the blooming period is fairly long. The down-curving (reflexed) parts show conspicuous veining and are noticeably lighter in color.

At first glance, the flower seems to have nine petals of varying sizes. However, three are petals, three are sepals, and three are petal-like branches of the style (female part of the flower). These branches of the style arch over the stamens, preventing self-pollination. The broad sepals are down-curving and have a yellow or amber midrib that ends in a hairy, bright yellow splotch at the base. This yellow area probably serves as a visual attractant for insects, thus ensuring pollination. The petals are more erect, narrower, and shorter than the showy sepals. When in bud, the flower is enclosed in two papery bracts.

The fruit is a three-lobed capsule, 1½ inches long at maturity, with many flat seeds in a row in each segment.

Native Americans used blueflag iris to treat earache, sore eyes, respiratory problems, and liver ailments. Pioneers learned to pound the root into a pulp and apply it as a dressing to relieve the swelling and pain of bruises and sores. Early pioneer medical practitioners sometimes utilized the unpleasant flavor of the root to induce vomiting or to "cleanse the intestines."

The French royal emblem (fleur-de-lis) represents the iris, but the exact derivation is obscure. A legend tells that King Clovis was unsuccessful in battle as long as the emblem on his shield had three black toads. From a holy hermit, Queen Clotilde learned about a shield, alleged to be as bright as the sun, with irises as the emblem. She convinced the king to change his emblem from toads to irises. After doing so, he became successful in battle.

photograph by Randall A. Maas

Other common names: needle-and-thread, needle grass (also applied to other species)

Stipa: from Greek *stype* for "tow," referring to the awns, which somewhat resemble the fibers of jute or flax when they are ready for spinning

Spartea: from Latin, meaning "broomlike"

Grass family: Poaceae (Gramineae)

Found mostly in the northern part of the tallgrass prairie and the Great Plains. Often it is in drier areas and in association with the bluestems. Flowers in May and June.

Stout, smooth, unbranched stems grow 1 to 4 feet tall. This cool season bunchgrass occurs in small clumps that are usually less than 4 inches across. It starts to grow in the fall and may remain green all winter. Most of its growth occurs by early June, with seeds developing in late June and maturing in early July. The plant remains more or less dormant during the summer.

The perennial root system extends deep into the soil. Reproduction is by seed and by extensive tillering.

Leaves along the stem range from 4 to 16 inches long. Basal leaves are from less than 1 foot to more than 2½ feet long. Leaves are mostly ⅛ to nearly ¼ inch wide and taper toward the tip. The underside is ribbed and the upper side is smooth. Leaves are flat but tend to roll up and become straw-colored as they dry out in midsummer. The leaf sheaths are longer than internodes of the stem.

A few sparse branches, individually 3 to 6 inches long, make up the loose, narrow flower head. The total flower head may be 10 or more inches long and may be erect or nodding. A few seed-producing spikelets are borne toward the tip of each branch. Glumes, 1 to 1½ inches long, are left in the head when the seeds drop.

Rigid and rough awns are a distinguishing feature of this species. Awn length is about 4 inches, sometimes as much as 8 inches. Typically, these slender, threadlike awns have two bends and are tightly spiraled toward the base.

Upon separation from the stem, the seeds have a needle-sharp point with short, stiff hairs that serve as barbs. When the seeds drop, they fall seed downward into the prairie vegetation. As the awn gets wet, it turns in one direction, and as it dries out, it turns in the other. Wetting and drying action allows the seed to "screw" itself through the vegetation and into the soil.

Unfortunately, in this same manner, the seeds may also work through the wool and into the flesh of sheep, thereby reducing their carcass value. Seeds have been known to work into the eyes, mouths, and noses of livestock that grazed on the plant when the seeds were dropping. This grass, however, is good grazing before the seed stage and after the seeds have dropped.

The Omaha and the Ponca called this grass *mika-hi* for "comb plant." The Pawnee called it *pitsuts* for "hairbrush." The stiff awns were bound into a bundle and the grains were burned off, leaving a brush for the hair. This brush was also used in some ceremonies.

photograph by John Schwegman

Other common names: cleavers, catchweed, goosegrass, burr-head, gripgrass, loveman, scratchweed, sweethearts, love-me-plant, beggar's lice, fleaweed, inchweed, pigtails, poor robin

Galium: from Greek for "milk," referring to the use of some species to curdle milk for cheesemaking

Species: There are at least 25 species of *Galium,* some of which are found in many different parts of the world. Two bedstraws are fairly common on Midwest prairies: northern bedstraw, *Galium boreale* (shown), and cleavers, *G. aparine.*

Madder family: Rubiaceae

Found on Midwest prairies, as well as in woods and woodland edges. Flowering is from May through June.

These rather inconspicuous plants with small white flowers often sprawl along the ground or climb on other plants. The fine stems of this genus are often weak and sprawling, especially in annual species. Most stems are four-angled. Some species have distinct bristles and hairy joints. The stems may be profusely branched. Their height varies from a few inches to 4 feet or more. *G. boreale,* a glabrous perennial with a conspicuous terminal panicle, grows erect, while *G. aparine,* a weak annual with axillary cymes, has a sprawling growth habit and is covered with hooked bristles.

The leaves occur in whorls of four or sometimes of six to eight. They are usually slender and pointed or tapered at each end, and they often have rough margins and midribs.

The flowers are inconspicuous and often go unnoticed. They are usually white but vary to greenish or yellow. The tiny, saucer-shaped flowers are about ⅛ inch across. They are usually found in loose clusters of three or fewer flowers on stalks from upper leaf axils. The flowers usually have four petals, but a few species have three. Though the plant and flowers are hardly noticeable, bristles on the fruit and plant parts tend to stick to clothing and can become quite a nuisance.

Young bedstraw plants have been used as greens. Seeds have served as a coffee substitute—the coffee plant is a member of this family. Leaves have been used to curdle milk for making cheese. Roots of *G. tinctorium* were a source of red-purple dye.

Medicinal capabilities once attributed to bedstraw include easing childbirth, slowing the flow of blood, increasing urine flow, stimulating the appetite, alleviating skin rashes, soothing nerves, correcting vitamin C deficiencies, reducing fever, and when used as a wash, removing freckles.

As the name bedstraw implies, these plants were once used as a filler for homemade mattresses. Because bristles tended to make the branches stick together, the mattress remained a uniform thickness. *G. verum,* with sweet-scented yellow flowers, was especially desirable for mattresses. Legend tells that the manger where the Christ Child was born contained this species of bedstraw. Folklore tells that if a newly married couple filled their mattress with bedstraw, they would be blessed with many children.

photograph by Ted Van Bruggen

Other common names: false indigo, bastard indigo, river locust

Amorpha: from Greek *amorphos,* meaning generally "without shape," referring to the flower with only one petal

Fruticosa: meaning "shrubby"

Legume family: Fabaceae (Leguminosae)

Found throughout the tallgrass biome on streambanks, along lakeshores, and in prairie swales. It is a heterogeneous plant with many varieties throughout its range. Blooming occurs from late May to July.

This shrub generally grows less than 10 feet high but may attain a height of 20 feet under ideal conditions. The long-petioled leaves are pubescent and pinnately compound with 13 to 35 leaflets that measure about 2 inches long and 1 inch wide. The leaflets have smooth margins, a grayish green cast, and large resinous dots.

The flower corolla consists of only the upper dilated petal called the standard, or banner. It is violet, usually ⅓ inch long, and wraps around the stamens and pistil. The inflorescence is a panicle of erect racemes, which gives it a spikelike appearance. The protruding anthers are a bright orange.

The curved seedpods, which also have large resinous dots, are less than ⅖ inch long. Although each pod contains only one or two seeds, the plant is prolific. The seeds are tiny, averaging 60,000 per pound.

The species was used medicinally, but the history of its uses has been lost through time. It is known that it was gathered and spread on the bison butchering ground to keep the meat clean.

Although the plant may be poisonous to stock that graze on it, it is a good wildlife food. It is valuable as a soil anchor along streams.

In some areas indigo bush is valued as an ornamental, but it does not survive well in shade. It is particularly attractive when in bloom.

Other members of the genus that occur in the tallgrass prairie are lead plant, *A. canescens,* and fragrant false indigo, *A. nana.* Both are 3 feet or less tall; lead plant is very hairy, while fragrant false indigo is glabrous (without hairs).

photograph by Tom Moore

Other common names: plains larkspur, prairie larkspur

Delphinium: Greek for "dolphin," referring to the shape of the flower

Virescens: meaning "greenish," referring to the greenish white flowers

Buttercup family: Ranunculaceae

Found in mesic areas throughout the tallgrass prairie region as well as in dry, open woodlands. Blooming from late May to July, its appearance is an early event on the prairie.

This erect perennial can grow singly or in clumps, the result of stems branching near the ground. Stems grow from 1 to 3 feet high. The plant is abundantly pubescent. The alternate leaves, 2 to 5 inches across, are mostly basal. They are palmately divided.

The flower head is a terminal raceme of creamy white or greenish white flowers tinged with a purplish spot. There are five petal-like sepals; the uppermost is elongated into a spur, which makes identification of the flower easy. There are four true petals; the lower two are bifid and bearded.

The fruit is a cylindrical follicle containing many small, brown, scale-covered seeds.

Because of its reputation as a poisonous plant, few medicinal uses of larkspur have been found. Dried seeds of various *Delphinium* species have been made into an ointment or lotion for destroying lice or itch mites.

All parts of the plant contain delphinine, which is poisonous to livestock. Although the dried plant seems to be harmless, western ranges that have relatively large populations of *Delphinium* are not safe for cattle unless the *Delphinium* is controlled or eliminated. Sheep may be used to graze such an area because the sheep are not as susceptible to the poison. Experiments have shown that sheep can be poisoned, but it takes about six times more plant material (on a percentage basis) to poison sheep than it does to poison cattle. Sheep usually do not eat enough to be severely poisoned.

This native perennial is one of the most handsome flowers on the prairie. It is familiar to many people because larkspurs are commonly grown in flower gardens. This species can be cultivated by sowing seeds in autumn or by subdividing the plant in spring.

photograph by Don Poggensee

Other common names: prairie blue-eyed grass

Sisyrinchium: a name once used for another plant and later transferred to this genus

Campestre: from Latin *campestre,* meaning "of the fields"

Iris family: Iridaceae

Found throughout the prairie and elsewhere, preferring sandy soils of open areas. Blooms May to June.

Tufts of smooth, leafless flowering stems grow to 18 inches tall but are usually less. These stems are less than ⅛ inch across; they are flattened and have two narrow ridges or wings. The root system is short and fibrous.

Smooth, linear, grasslike leaves arising from ground level are only slightly wider than the stems. They are a distinctive pale green color. These leaves stand more or less erect and are often taller than the flowerstems.

The petals and sepals of blue-eyed grass are alike; they form a six-pointed, starlike flower that is usually ¼ to ½ inch across. Each "petal" is slightly broader toward its blunt, rounded outer end. The center of this end contains a sharp point that tends to curve slightly to one side. Although called blue-eyed grass, the color varies from white to pale blue with a yellow center, and of course, it is not a grass. Other forms of *Sisyrinchium* may have purple, violet, or even yellow flowers.

The fruit is a pea-sized, globose capsule with three segments. Each segment contains many tiny, roundish, black seeds. When this plant is not in bloom or in fruit, it is frequently mistaken for a grass.

A tea for stomach cramps has been prepared from *S. campestre.* Other species were boiled to make a tea for hay fever.

The Menomini used some species in their dwellings and on their persons to ward off snakes. They also mixed plants of this genus with oats to make horses fat and vicious—the horse's bite was supposed to be poisonous, but the horse would not bite the owner. The medicine man used this herb on horse bites to protect the victim.

The Meskwaki used it to make a medicine for treating piles and to make a mixture for a woman with an injured womb to drink.

Some species are used for ornamental purposes. It seeds easily and has a tendency to form small patches.

There are about 150 species in this genus—all of them in America. *S. augustifolium,* a related species, is found mostly in open woodlands and in moist soil along streams, less frequently in open prairie areas in the southern part of the tallgrass prairie.

photograph by Sylvan T. Runkel

Other common names: ragwort, groundsel, squaw-weed, prairie ragwort

Senecio: Latin name of a plant; from *senex,* "an old man," referring to the whitish cast of many species or to the white hairs of the pappus

Plattensis: named for the Platte River region

Daisy family: Asteraceae (Compositae)

Found on dry, calcareous bluffs, river valleys, and prairies throughout the tallgrass prairie biome. One of the early flowering events on the prairie, it blooms from May to early July.

Prairie groundsel is an erect perennial that has mainly basal leaves. These alternate, thick, and oval leaves are up to 4 inches long and have serrate margins. Especially when the plant is young, the undersides of the leaves are covered with a fine wool that forms a cottony layer.

Stem leaves are sparse; they are alternate, often deeply pinnately lobed, and linear or lance-shaped with a prominent toothed lobe at the tip. A good field identification characteristic is the contrast between the simple basal leaves and the pinnately divided stem leaves.

The flower heads, which can be up to ¾ inch across, are terminal; they are arranged in a loose, flat-topped inflorescence of up to 10 individual flowers. The ray and disk florets are yellow to yellow-orange.

The fruit is a smooth achene with a tuft of white hairs at the top and with hairs on the angles.

Plants of this genus, including the closely related *S. aureus* and *S. integerrimus,* were used to increase perspiration and to treat kidney stones and lung troubles. They were used by American Indian women for general health, hence, the name squaw-weed. They served as diuretics, diaphoretics, and tonics for early European settlers. (Because the plants are poisonous, one can speculate on the virtues compared to the dangers of their use.)

Plants of the genus *Senecio* are known to cause liver damage to grazing livestock. Afflicted animals may stagger, walk continuously, and become disoriented.

Consisting of over 1000 species, the genus *Senecio* is very large and widespread. There are over a dozen species in the tallgrass biome. Most species become abundant in overgrazed areas.

The golden ragwort, *S. aureus,* is very common in the tallgrass prairie region. It differs from prairie groundsel by being nearly glabrous (smooth, due to a lack of hairs), growing in a more moist habitat, and having heart-shaped basal leaves.

Another groundsel, *S. integerrimus,* is widespread on the Great Plains. It has mostly entire or merely denticulate leaves; the basal leaves are much larger than the rapidly decreasing and slender upper ones. The species name *integerrimus,* which means "mostly entire," refers to the leaf margins.

The ragworts are showy members of the prairie flora; their appearance is a welcome event on the drab-colored spring prairie landscape.

photograph by Ted Van Bruggen

Other common names: shell-leaf penstemon, wild foxglove, Canterbury bells, showy beardtongue, pink beardtongue

Penstemon: from Greek, meaning "five stamens"

Grandiflorus: meaning "large-flowered"

Snapdragon family: Scrophulariaceae

Found throughout the western part of the tallgrass prairie biome, in suitable habitats into Wisconsin and Illinois, and in areas where it has escaped from cultivation. It needs sandy or well-drained soils such as loess. Large-flowered beardtongue blooms in late May and early June, providing one of the spectacular events of the prairie year.

This handsome perennial species may achieve a height of 3 feet. The opposite leaves are thick and fleshy, entire and clasping or perfoliate; they have a distinctive waxy blue sheen. The spatulate basal leaves are in a clump; stem leaves are progressively shorter with increasing height on the stem.

The root system is rather shallow and does not spread by rhizomes.

The large, 2-inch, pale purple flowers are five-lobed and short-lived; the corollas fall easily. As many as 12 blossoms may be present on one plant. Beardtongues are so named because one of the five stamens is sterile, long, and hairy, resembling a "bearded tongue." *P. grandiflorus* is only minutely bearded at the apex of the "tongue." Observation of the fifth stamen as being

uniquely bearded is generally a good confirmation of the identity of the beardtongues, or penstemons.

Seed capsules are up to ½ inch long and contain many seeds.

Native Americans treated toothache by chewing the root pulp of plants in this genus and placing it in the cavity. The Pawnee used a decoction of the leaves, taken internally, as a remedy for chills and fever. The Navajo applied a wet dressing of pounded leaves of beardtongue to rattlesnake bites; they considered this an absolute antidote.

Rodents eat the seeds of penstemons. In range country, cobaea penstemon is readily eaten by all classes of livestock.

P. grandiflorus is one of the most beautiful prairie species, but it is very difficult to maintain in gardens.

Other *Penstemon* species add beauty and diversity to the prairie. Cobaea penstemon is one that is beautiful and widespread in the prairie, mainly east of the 30-inch rainfall belt. It produces purplish white flowers with dark purple stripes inside.

There are about 250 species of penstemons, and most of them are found in the United States. Many of them are difficult to identify individually, and as a group they may be confusing to many people.

photograph by Randall A. Maas

Other common names: none known

Penstemon: from Greek *penta,* meaning "five," and *stemon,* meaning "stamen"

Pallidus: meaning "pale"

Snapdragon family: Scrophulariaceae

Found widespread in the eastern part of the tallgrass prairie, favoring sandy or loamy soils and occasionally growing on roadsides and in disturbed fields. It may also occur in dry, open woodlands. Blooms late May through July.

Pale beardtongue may grow to a height of 3 feet, although it is usually shorter. The stem is downy. The hairy, firm, leathery leaves up to ½ inch wide are opposite. The basal leaves have petioles, while the stem leaves are sessile.

The flowers, which are white with faint purple lines inside, are up to an inch long. They make this species an exceedingly attractive member of the prairie flora, but it pales in contrast to its large-flowered relative, *P. grandiflorus.* Arranged in a loose panicle, the flowers may number 20 on a single plant. As in other members of the genus, the corolla has an upper two-lobed lip and a lower three-cleft lip. It gets its common name, beardtongue, from the tufted, sterile stamen. This species has hairs along most of the length of the sterile stamen.

Pollination is by insects, and the resulting fruit is a capsule containing many seeds. Reproduction is by seed, although the plant is a weak perennial. It is especially difficult to get the plants established under cultivated conditions. Once established, however, it readily self-sows, and populations persist rather easily.

Native Americans have used plants of this genus as a remedy for chills and fever. To treat toothache, they chewed the root pulp and placed it in the painful cavity.

The large showy flowers of the beardtongues are one of the most spectacular early events of the prairie year. Other penstemons found on prairies include *P. digitalis,* foxglove beardtongue; *P. gracilis,* white-flowered beardtongue; *P. albidus; P. tubiflorus; P. cobaea,* cobaea penstemon; and *P. grandiflorus,* large-flowered beardtongue.

There are about 10 species found in the eastern United States, while more than 230 different species may be found in the southern, central, western, and northwestern parts of the continental United States and in Alaska.

photograph by John Schwegman

Other common names: crazyweed, Lambert crazyweed, stemless locoweed

Oxytropis: from Greek *oxys,* meaning "sharp," and *tropis,* meaning "keel," for the pointed keel of the flower, which distinguishes this genus from *Astragalus*

Lambertii: in honor of Aylmer Bourke Lambert, from whose living plant collection Pursh described this species

Legume family: Fabaceae (Leguminosae)

Found in dry, high-lime hillsides of the Great Plains and in the tallgrass prairie transition to mixed-grass prairie. Blooms from May through July.

Locoweed is short, growing only 6 to 12 inches tall. One to several clustered crowns arise from a single, woody taproot that may penetrate 8 feet into the soil.

Rather stiff, leathery leaves 4 to 9 inches long usually have 9 to 23 leaflets oppositely arranged along a central petiole. Leaflets are narrow, egg-shaped, ½ to 1 inch long, and generally less than ¼ inch wide. The leaves all arise from ground level rather than from an aboveground stem. Both leaves and flowerstalks are covered with fine, silky hairs.

Tufts of flowerstalks as tall as 12 inches arise from among the clumps of leaves. The top 1 to 6 inches of this stalk carries a spike of 10 to 25 sweet-scented, pea-like flowers.

The upper lip of the legume flower, called a banner, tends to turn upward. The lower lip, or keel, is distinctly pointed, unlike *Astragalus,* which has a rounded keel. These flowers, each about ¾ inch long, are mostly purple but sometimes white or light yellow. A single colony of plants may contain both colors of flowers.

The fruit is a leathery, cylindrical pod with a sharp beak at its tip. The pod is hairy, slightly curved, and mostly erect. These pods are generally ½ to ¾ inch long and have few seeds.

Although locoweed is unpalatable, it is sometimes eaten by livestock, usually when a pasture is overgrazed early in the season. Livestock sometimes become addicted to this plant, but relatively large amounts must be eaten to produce a dangerous level of poison in the system. The effects are cumulative, occurring slowly and progressing over weeks or months. In the early stages of poisoning, horses may spook easily and run into objects, as if they have faulty vision. Other effects are trembling, depression, and paralysis—even to the degree that the animals may die. Sick animals must be removed from the plant source.

photograph by Don Poggensee

Other common names: marbleseed

Onosmodium: named for its likeness to the genus *Onosma* — a word that means "smell of a donkey"

Occidentale: from the Latin *occidentalis,* meaning "western." This refers to the fact that, unlike *O. hispidissimum,* which is also found in the area, this species does not range east of the tallgrass prairie.

Forget-me-not family: Boraginaceae

Found throughout the tallgrass prairie and westward, especially in drier areas with sandy, gravelly, or rocky soils. Flowers late May through July.

This coarse plant bristles with stiff hairs. The stem grows erect, 1 to 3 feet tall, often with some branching toward the top.

Leaves, without petioles, attach alternately along the stem. They are generally about 2 inches long and have five to seven prominent rib veins. They vary from oval to lance-shaped and have smooth margins. Leaves, as well as the stem, take on a grayish tint from the dense covering of hairs.

As is typical of the Boraginaceae (forget-me-not family), the flowers are borne along the outer side of a gracefully curved spike. Their color varies from a dirty greenish white to yellowish. Five sharp-pointed petals join to form a tube from which projects a long, threadlike style (a female flower part). The flower is usually ½ to ¾ inch long.

The flower is unique in that the stigma (a female flower part) protrudes through the closed corolla. Apparently the flower is fertilized and the reproduction process is completed before the flower opens its corolla.

The oval nutlets, about ⅛ inch long, are dull, whitish, and smooth. They are not constricted toward the base as they are in *O. hispidissimum* and most other species. The small nutlets are very hard, which may account for the common name marbleseed.

Roots and leaves of this species have been used to make a liniment to treat swelling in horses and humans.

Some people say this plant smells like a wet dog; others say that it smells like a donkey. Animal lovers who are allergic to animals might enjoy living near the false gromwell.

There are about 10 species of *Onosmodium* in North and South America.

photograph by Tomma Lou Maas

Other common names: licorice root, American licorice, sweet wood

Glycyrrhiza: from Greek *glycys,* meaning "sweet," and *rhiza,* meaning "root"

Lepidota: meaning "scaled" or "scaly"

Legume family: Fabaceae (Leguminosae)

Found throughout the Great Plains and prairies and west to the Pacific coast, and to the east. Wild licorice occurs on prairies, pastures, meadows, lakeshores, railroad rights-of-way, and other disturbed areas. Blooms May to August.

This erect, perennial herb has a rather coarse stem that may reach up to 3 feet. The stem is covered with minute, sticky hairs. The plant's deep and spreading roots often penetrate more than 5 feet into the prairie soil.

Leaves are alternate and pinnately compound. The 11 to 19 oblong or lanceolate, entire leaflets have glandular dots on the undersides. Leaflets are 1 to 1½ inches long.

The yellowish white flowers, which resemble those of alfalfa, are on a crowded terminal spike. The five petals are spreading or curved backward; the calyx is four-toothed.

The brown fruit is less than an inch long and is elliptic in shape. Covered with hooked spines, it resembles a small cocklebur. The spines make the fruits easily dispersed; this has led to the plant's establishment in many sites out of its normal range. Reproduction is by seed and underground rootstalks.

Medicinally, an extract of wild licorice roots has served as an expectorant. A root decoction has been used to induce menstrual flow, treat fevers in nursing mothers, and help promote the expulsion of afterbirth. The Blackfoot steeped the leaves in water and drank the liquid to treat earaches. This plant was also used as a purgative, as a blood clotting agent, and as a treatment for inflamed membranes and stomach ulcers.

This plant is the counterpart of the cultivated European licorice plant. The root, which has a distinct licorice flavor, was popular with American Indians, who ate it raw or roasted it in ashes. Sometimes the plant was cultivated by the Indians. Pioneers chewed the root for its flavor, and it has been used as a flavoring in medicine, candy, root beers, and chewing tobacco.

The burs have gotten in the wool of sheep, so the plant has been listed as a weed in some areas.

Commercial licorice is obtained from another plant of this genus, *G. glabra,* which is not native to this country.

photograph by LeRoy G. Pratt

Other common names: small white lady slipper, ducks

Cypripedium: an incorrectly Latinized version of ancient Greek words meaning generally "Venus's shoe"

Candidum: from Latin, meaning "white"

Orchid family: Orchidaceae

Found in wet prairies and meadows throughout the Midwest and Northeast. High-lime areas are preferred. Flowers from May through July.

The stiff, green stems of the little white orchid are usually 6 to 18 inches tall. They grow from a perennial rootstock that is coarsely fibrous and fleshy.

The three to five basal leaves, shaped as narrow ovals with pointed tips, sheath the stem and stand mostly erect. The leaves are up to 5 inches long and 1½ inches across.

One, rarely two, slightly fragrant flowers per stem are typical of this lady slipper. The sepals and petals are greenish yellow, often with purple spots. The upper sepal is narrow, about 1 inch long; the lateral pair of sepals is united nearly to the tip. Larger than the sepals, the lateral petals are narrow and twisted, perhaps 1½ inches long. The lower petal is pouchlike, ½ to 1 inch long, and waxy white, with red or purple stripes inside the pouch. Narrow, lance-shaped bracts 1 to 2 inches long are at the base of the flower.

The fruit is three-angled and consists of a single cell. It contains numerous tiny, spindle-shaped seeds.

Cypripediums are considered sedative, antispasmodic, nerve medicines, with "all species considered equally medicinal." Early practitioners used a teaspoon of the powdered root dissolved in sugar water to treat insomnia.

Glandular hairs on the stems and leaves of cypripediums contain a toxic substance that causes a skin reaction in many people, especially in hot weather when they perspire.

This diminutive orchid enters the tallgrass biome from the east and seems to be decreasing throughout its range. Its relatively short blooming time and restricted habitat make finding it in the prairie swale a memorable event. It sometimes hybridizes with the yellow lady slipper.

Because of the special growing conditions they require, all lady slippers should be enjoyed but left where they are found unless they are physically threatened or in imminent danger of destruction.

photograph by William P. Pusateri

Other common names: umbrellawort

Mirabilis: from Latin for "wonderful" or "strange." The genus name was once *Admirabilis,* but it was shortened by Linnaeus. (Carolus Linnaeus was the Swedish naturalist and botanist who established the modern method of applying genus and species names to all plants and animals. His book *Species Plantarum,* published in 1753, provides the basis for plant classification.)

Nyctaginea: from Greek, indirectly meaning "nightblooming"

Four o'clock family: Nyctaginaceae

Found throughout the tallgrass prairie region in prairies, roadsides, open woodlands, and woodland edges. Blooms May through August.

Nearly smooth, reddish stems vary from 1 foot to over 4 feet tall and are squarish in cross section. They are profusely forked, especially near the top, and are covered with leaves.

The leaves are opposite and have smooth margins and short petioles. They are more or less heart-shaped, growing to 4 inches long and 3 inches wide. Uppermost leaves are often quite small, appearing more like bracts than leaves.

The root system of this perennial is a thick, fleshy taproot.

Pink to purple bell-shaped flowers up to ⅜ inch across face upward in tight, flat-topped terminal clusters. The flower clusters arise from the uppermost forks of the stem branches. As many as five flowers are seated upon a shallow, green, cup-shaped platform that is five-lobed and perhaps ¾ inch across.

Five showy sepals give the flowers their color, since four o'clocks have no true petals. The sepals are joined to form a spreading bell that is fluted or pleated. The flare of the bell has five shallow notches. The flowers open in late afternoon, giving rise to the common name four o'clock.

Fruits are hairy capsules containing tiny, hard nutlets that are about ⅙ inch long. The nutlets are brown, angular, and five-ribbed. Membrane-like bracts with prominent veining enlarge during fruiting and persist late in the season.

The Navajo mixed dried and powdered native four o'clock with sheep fat and red ochre as a treatment for burns. Other American Indians pounded the root to make a poultice for relieving swellings, sprains, and burns. A brew of the roots was used for controlling internal parasites. A frequent treatment for bladder trouble was a tea made from the roots or from the whole plant. In the West, American Indians used a closely related species in many ways, including the inducement of visions.

Whether early European settlers found uses for wild four o'clock plants is not known.

A close relative, the common four o'clock of flower gardens, is a foreign introduction, whereas the wild four o'clock is a native species.

photograph by Ted Van Bruggen

Other common names: American feverfew, feverfew

Parthenium: from Greek *parthenos,* for "virgin," referring to the infertile disk flowers. It is also the Greek name for another plant.

Integrifolium: from Latin, meaning "entire-leaved"

Daisy family: Asteraceae (Compositae)

Found in dry areas of prairies and open woods over much of the United States east of the shortgrass areas of the Great Plains. Blooms May to September.

Stems up to 4 feet tall arise from a short, thickened, tuberous rootstock. The large basal leaves on long petioles may be up to 12 inches long and 4 inches wide. They are rough and hairy on the upper surface and sometimes on the lower surface as well.

Leaves along the stem are alternate and become progressively smaller toward the top. Petioles of stem leaves also become progressively shorter, with top leaves having no petiole and even clasping the stem.

The leaves are long ovals that are somewhat pointed at the tips. The margins have coarse, rounded teeth. These teeth are so coarse on the lower leaves that they may appear as lobes and may have toothed edges themselves.

The flower heads are flat-topped, multibranched clusters that some people have described as looking somewhat similar to a head of cauliflower. Individual whitish flowers are about ¼ inch high and somewhat globular in shape. The flowers of the center disk are sterile. Five tiny ray flowers are spaced around the disk in daisy-like fashion. The flower nestles in two or three rows of short, rounded bracts.

The fertile ray flowers produce tiny black seeds that are less than ⅛ inch long. The seeds are flattened, with thin margins and a ridge on one side. The outer tip often has two or three scales or tiny awns.

A tea of the leaves has been used to treat fevers, giving rise to the common names wild quinine and feverfew. The Catawba placed fresh leaves on burns.

A related species, guayule (*P. argentatum*), found in Mexico and Texas was used as a minor source of rubber during World War II. Because of the war, supplies of rubber from Asia and Africa were at risk of being cut off, so there was great interest in finding a local source. Guayule was a possible rubber source that was investigated as a farm crop. Interest waned, however, when the commercial process for making rubber was perfected.

photograph by Sylvan T. Runkel

Other common names: false mallow, red false mallow, cowboy's delight, prairie mallow, copper mallow, flame mallow

Sphaeralcea: from the Greek *sphaira,* "a sphere," and *alcea,* "a mallow"; a name derived from the spherical fruit

Coccinea: meaning "scarlet"

Mallow family: Malvaceae

Found on dry, sandy plains and loess prairies from Manitoba to western Iowa to Texas and westward, the scarlet globe mallow blooms from May to August.

This low-growing, branched perennial may grow to a height of 1 foot. It has alternate leaves that are deeply three-parted; the divisions commonly are lobed.

The leaves and stems are covered with starlike, branched, grayish hairs that are visible with a hand lens. These hairs give the plant a grayish appearance.

Clustered in short, leafy racemes, the flowers range in color from red to salmon and are accented by creamy yellow stamen columns. Petals are about ¾ inch in length.

The fruit is a spherical capsule of 10 or more densely hairy carpels, each with one seed. However, the plant spreads by creeping roots.

The Plains Indians chewed the scarlet globe mallow plant to prepare a poultice for wounds. The plant also was chewed to a paste that was applied to the skin of the hands and arms so that they could be thrust into very hot water. This normally was of use only to medicine men.

In some parts of the arid West, this species is considered an important grazing plant. It has the ability to drop its leaves during a severe drought. When the rains return, new leaves grow, making this one of the most drought-resistant of prairie plants. This unusual quality also may account for one of its common names—cowboy's delight.

There are about 50 species of *Sphaeralcea* worldwide. About 6 species may be found in the Rocky Mountains, but plants of this genus are principally plants of the Great Plains; they barely reach the tallgrass biome. They can exist in harsh environments and in disturbed habitats, such as roadsides, and they provide color in the prairie landscape.

The mallow family has many flower species that have been widely planted in flower gardens. The hollyhock is one of the old favorites. The prominent pistil column of its flower shows that the scarlet globe mallow is a relative of the hollyhock.

There are also some species in the mallow family that are economically important as agricultural crops. Cotton and okra, both members of the mallow family, are widely grown.

One of the largest of our wildflowers is a mallow—the rose mallow, which has a flower that sometimes is 6 inches or more in diameter.

photograph by William P. Pusateri

Other common names: beargrass, grass cactus, small soapweed, soap root, Spanish bayonet

Yucca: the native Haitian name for this genus

Glauca: from Greek, meaning generally "grayish or bluish green"

Lily family: Liliaceae (sometimes Agavaceae)

Found in dry, well-drained soils of the Great Plains and the western edge of the midwestern prairie. Blooms early June to July.

The leaves of this large plant all arise from the base. They are stiff and bayonet-like but smooth except for whitish marginal hairs that are long and threadlike. The perennial evergreen leaves may be 3 feet long but are seldom more than ½ inch wide. These thick leaves are rounded on the underside; incurved margins give them a slightly concave upper surface.

The stout flowerstalk grows to 6 feet tall. Large, nodding, bell-shaped flowers on short, individual branches of the main stalk grow in a spikelike manner. Three petals and three similar sepals are a white to greenish color, oval to lance-shaped, and up to 1½ inches long. Flowers may be 3 inches across.

The fruit is a six-sided, three-celled, dry, brown capsule containing many flat, black seeds. Seed production depends on the pronuba moth, a small silvery moth that gathers a ball of pollen and places it on the stigma, ensuring pollination. But the moth also lays its eggs in the developing seed capsules, where a row or two of seeds will provide food for the larvae. Neither the yucca nor the moth would survive without the other.

This genus also reproduces from a thickened underground stem, so it frequently occurs in colonies.

The dried pulp of the fruit of some species was a mainstay of Navajo warriors when they journeyed great distances. If picked while green and then roasted, the pods tasted something like sweet potatoes. Sliced pulp of nearly ripe pods was used to make "apple" pie. Pulp was boiled into a paste, rolled into sheets up to 1 inch thick, dried, and cut into pieces for storage. The fruit also was baked, peeled, and eaten.

Flower petals were used in salads, and the older flowers were eaten raw or boiled. Flowerstalks were eaten when full grown but before the buds expanded. Stalks were cooked in sections and then the rind was removed.

Roots produce a good lather when cut, mashed, and rubbed vigorously in water. As soap, it leaves the skin soft and not dry. American Indians used this soap for washing hair; the Kiowa treated dandruff and skin irritations with it. Among the Hopi, a treatment for balding was to coat the remaining hair with soapweed and rub in duck grease (because ducks have heavy coatings of feathers). A commercial soap (Aniole) was made from yucca. The Cherokee used the roots to make a poultice and salves.

Leaves were mashed until the fibers could be separated. The fibers were twined into thread that, with the sharp, hard points of the leaves still attached to serve as needles, was used for sewing and basket weaving. The fibers also served as rope and were woven into mats.

photograph by Sylvan T. Runkel

Other common names: red root, mountain sweet, wild snowball, wild pepper, spangles, walpalo tea

Ceanothus: an ancient name, the meaning of which is lost in antiquity

Americanus: meaning "of America"

Buckthorn family: Rhamnaceae

Found throughout prairies and prairie relicts and also along borders of woods, commonly on gravelly or rocky sites. Blooms late May to September.

New Jersey tea is a low, upright shrub that may be up to 3 feet high. Usually several branching stems arise from the deep red root. The entire plant has a gray-green cast.

Toothed, alternate leaves are from 1 to 3 inches long and ½ to 1 inch wide. Leaves are pubescent, especially underneath, and have three prominent veins.

The small, hooded, five-petaled flowers occur in dense, oblong clusters at the end of the fruiting stems. These clusters are from about ¾ to 1½ inches in diameter. Each flower has a stem, ¼ to ½ inch long, that is the current year's new growth.

The dry, three-lobed fruit splits into three parts when it is dry and mature.

Native Americans ascribed great powers to New Jersey tea, calling it *kituki manito,* meaning "spotted snake spirit." Its twisted, intricately knotted roots reminded them of bowels, so they considered it good for bowel troubles. A decoction of leaves and seeds was used to cure ulcerated sore throats. This plant was also used to treat gonorrhea, dysentery, eye trouble in children, and high blood pressure. It served as a stimulant, a sedative, an expectorant, and an astringent.

Among our native plants, it is probably the best-known substitute for tea. Leaves, gathered while plants were in full bloom, were dried and stored like other tea plants. New Jersey tea contains no caffeine, but objectionable alkaloids may be extracted if it is steeped too long.

Because of the English tax on tea, the colonists boycotted the tea that was shipped in. During the Revolutionary War, New Jersey tea was considered the best tea substitute.

New Jersey tea was used to tan hides because its root and bark are very high in tannin.

When they are crushed and rubbed in water, the fresh flowers of some species make excellent lather. The Cherokee used the lather as a wash for skin cancer and venereal sores.

Another species provided a dye that gave wool a cinnamon color.

A related species, *C. ovatus,* is a far-ranging member of the prairie flora. It has narrow, elliptic leaves, and the peduncles that terminate the branches are shorter than those of *C. americanus.*

C. americanus and *C. ovatus* were both commonly called red root by the early settlers. Both were considered very tough obstacles to plowing the original prairie. Their deep taproots are capable of fixing nitrogen.

photograph by LeRoy G. Pratt

Other common names: Virginia ground cherry, old squaw berry, tomatos del campo, husk tomatoes

Physalis: from Greek, meaning "bladder," referring to the bladderlike husk of the fruit

Virginiana: meaning "of Virginia"

Nightshade family: Solanaceae

Found throughout the eastern United States in dry woodlands, field edges, and in somewhat disturbed or sandy parts of dry prairies. This plant has a wide ecological tolerance. It has a long flowering time, from late May to August.

The ground cherry may achieve a height of 1½ feet, but it is usually closer to a foot tall. The forked stem is covered with rather long hairs. Stalked leaves, which are several times as long as they are broad, taper at both ends.

This perennial plant arises from a deep rhizome, which allows it to form small colonies.

Flowers are bell-shaped. The dull yellow corolla has a brown center that is ½ inch wide.

When in fruit, the calyx is sunken at the base and is much larger than the reddish berry. The berry is edible when it is thoroughly ripe in late summer and fall and is completely enclosed in a papery husk that resembles a miniature Japanese lantern.

Ground cherries were sometimes used as a poultice for snakebites. A tea brewed from the plant was said to cure dropsy.

The Meskwaki prepared a tea from the whole plant and used it as a cure for dizziness.

American Indians and pioneers ate ground cherries raw or cooked. The cooked form was usually sauce in the case of Indians, pies or preserves in the case of pioneers. The ground cherry is still cultivated in gardens, and sometimes the fruits are sold in markets.

Insects, birds, and rodents find ground cherry fruits a favorite source of late fall nutrition, but their overall wildlife value is small.

Other species that may be found on disturbed prairie sites include *P. heterophylla,* which has sticky hairs and a yellow berry and is somewhat taller. *P. lanceolata* has lance-shaped or triangular leaves and yellow, green, or reddish berries with a calyx that is not sunken at the base.

Although the nightshade family has some poisonous members, it also includes some of our more important vegetable foods: tomatoes, potatoes, eggplants, and red and green peppers.

photograph by LeRoy G. Pratt

Other common names: no other known English names

Gaura: from Greek, meaning "superb"

Parviflora: from Latin, meaning "small flower"

Evening primrose family: Onagraceae

Found from Indiana to Washington and south to Louisiana, Texas, New Mexico, and Mexico, it favors dry prairies and fields. Besides *G. parviflora,* there are three or more other species of *Gaura* that may be found on the tallgrass prairie, in fields, and on roadsides. They include annuals, biennials, and perennials. Blooms May to October.

Small-flowered gaura may grow to 6 feet tall as an erect, branched plant with a whitish pubescence. The long, oval to lance-shaped leaves, which narrow toward the base, are 1½ to 4 inches long and ⅓ inch to 1½ inches wide. The leaves are lightly dusted with a whitish pubescence. There is one form, *G. glabra,* that is quite smooth, with little or no pubescence.

The pink petals of *G. parviflora* are less than ¹⁄₁₀ inch long, and the entire flower is only about ⅙ inch across, making it truly a small flower, as in the name parviflora. The petals of all *Gaura* species do not appear to go completely around the center part of the flower, so the flowers look somewhat unbalanced or irregular. There usually are eight protruding stamens.

The flowering parts of *Gaura* species show their relationship to the evening primrose by having four petals and a pistil with a cross-shaped tip. Flowers of the evening primrose family are known to vary in color as they age, and sometimes a single plant will have some flowers with pure white color and others with deep pink color. *Gaura* species have somewhat similar characteristics. The flowers of scarlet gaura (*G. coccinea*), also called butterfly weed, open as pure white petals; however, as the sun warms them, they gradually turn pink and finally become deep scarlet. Flowers ranging from pure white to blazing scarlet may be found on the same stalk.

The flower of *G. parviflora* develops into a sessile, podlike, four-angled fruit that is about ⅓ inch long. It does not open. Some authorities describe it as a "kind of nut."

Some American Indians are said to have used scarlet gaura "to catch horses with." They chewed it, then rubbed the resulting mixture on their hands. It is not known how effective this was in catching horses!

Scarlet gaura is much smaller than small-flowered gaura; it grows to only a few inches high in some areas but to as much as 3 feet in others. It is a perennial that has a very deep, spreading root system. Reproduction is from the root as well as by seed. To some people, the scarlet gaura flower appears similar to a spider; to others, a butterfly. The flowers are in spikes, but since they bloom from the bottom up, only a few flowers are in bloom at one time. Bright flowers with an outstandingly sweet fragrance make it an excellent plant in wildflower gardens.

G. biennis, which is much-branched and completes its life cycle in two years, is another common species in some areas.

photograph by Don Poggensee

Other common names: ten-petaled blazing star, prairie lily, sand lily

Stickleaf mentzelia: *Mentzelia oligosperma* Nutt.

Other common names: few-seeded mentzelia, five-petaled mentzelia

Mentzelia: named in honor of Christian Mentzel, a German botanist of the late 17th century

Decapetala: from Latin, meaning "ten petals"

Oligosperma: from Latin, meaning "few-seeded," for this characteristic of the species

Loasa family: Loasaceae

Found scattered throughout the western portion of the tallgrass prairie and Great Plains, usually on the high-lime soils of dry hillsides. *M. decapetala* blooms June to September; *M. oligosperma* blooms May to July.

These erect, multibranched perennials have straw-colored stems that are covered with barbed hairs. Stems grow 1 to 3 feet tall. The roots are spindle-shaped, thickening toward the middle.

The coarsely toothed, alternate leaves sometimes have wavy margins. They are 1 to 3 inches long. Leaves on the upper part of the plant do not have petioles, and they are rounded toward the base. The lower leaves are narrowed toward the base. Coarse, barbed hairs cover the leaves. These hairs cause the leaves to stick to clothing.

The flowers of *M. decapetala* open at dusk. Its flowers have 10 lanceolate, pale yellow petals. Its elongate leaves are sharply and coarsely dentate.

The colorful yellow flowers of *M. oligosperma* open only in bright sunshine; they have five wedge-shaped petals that spread to give a flattened appearance to the flower. Individual petals may be as long as ½ inch. The linear, green sepals are only about half as long as the petals. The scattered flowers are borne at the tips of stems that arise from the upper leaf axils.

M. decapetala is pollinated by moths and other night-flying insects, while *M. oligosperma* is pollinated by day-flying insects.

The fruit is a small, single-celled capsule no more than ½ inch long. The capsule opens at the tip when it is dry. In *M. decapetala,* the capsule contains numerous seeds; in *M. oligosperma,* it contains up to nine seeds.

The fruit of *M. decapetala* is sometimes parched and ground into a nutritious meal.

Another species, *M. nuda,* was introduced from the west. Its stems were pounded to extract a gummy, yellow juice, which was boiled and strained, then applied externally to reduce fever.

photograph by Jean Novacek

Other common names: rush skeleton plant, skeleton plant, prairie pink

Lygodesmia: from Greek *lygos,* meaning "a pliant twig," and *desme,* meaning "a bundle," from the fascicled twiglike appearance of the plant

Juncea: meaning stiff, like a rush

Daisy family: Asteraceae (Compositae)

Found principally in the Great Plains, east to western Iowa and occasionally to Wisconsin. It prefers dry, disturbed ground. Blooming occurs from June into August or later.

The perennial plant body grows to a height of about 1 foot. The nearly leafless, greenish gray herbaceous stem is much branched; it is inconspicuous when not in flower. The leaves, especially the upper ones, are reduced to small lance-shaped structures less than ½ inch long.

Because several species of insects lay their eggs on its stem, this plant is nearly always infested with insect galls that can be up to pea-size. (In the accompanying photo, the white spot on the stem is the froth of a spittle bug, not an insect gall.)

The roots penetrate deeply, perhaps to a depth of 20 feet. Reproduction of skeleton weed is by seed; there is no vegetative spreading by rhizome because the root system is so deep. It is one of the first plants to colonize a recently eroded site, especially in a loess soil.

The five-parted, pale pink to nearly white flower occurs as a terminal, solitary blossom. Flowers are sparsely distributed on the plant.

Native Great Plains peoples soaked the stems of skeleton weed to make an infusion they used as a treatment for sore eyes. Nursing mothers drank the mixture to increase the flow of milk.

In regions where rosinweed did not occur, this plant was used as a source of chewing gum. The stems were gathered and cut into pieces. The cut stems exuded a material that, when hardened, was collected for chewing. When chewed, this exudate soon turns a bright blue color. Mexican children are reported to have also used this plant for chewing gum.

Skeleton weed is a good example of a plant adaptation to extremely dry conditions. By being nearly leafless, the green herbaceous stems reduce water loss but at the same time carry on photosynthesis. Because the roots penetrate the soil so deeply, the plant is very drought-hardy.

Since the herbage is distasteful to range animals, the palatability of skeleton weed is low, but in dry regions sheep will graze it. In some areas it has been suspected of being poisonous.

photograph by Sylvan T. Runkel

Other common names: Virginia bunchflower

Melanthium: from the Greek *melas,* meaning "black," and *anthos,* meaning "flower"

Virginicum: meaning "Virginian" or "of Virginia"

Lily family: Liliaceae

Found on low prairies, carex meadows, savannas, and wet woods from the southern United States north to New York, Minnesota, and Indiana. Flowering time is June and July.

This attractive perennial may achieve a height of over 4 feet. The stem is stout and erect and arises from a thick rhizome. The stem and inflorescence are pubescent.

The leaves are linear. The lower ones are elongate, achieving a length of over a foot and a width of less than an inch, and they form a sheath at the base. The upper leaves are short and grasslike.

Flowers are borne in a loose panicle that may become nearly 2 feet in length. Individual flowers are cream-colored, changing to a green, purplish, or blackish color with age. (This is the basis of the scientific name.) Individual flowers may be nearly an inch across. They have two dark glands (visible with a hand lens) at the base of each segment. The sepals and petals total six and are similar. They narrow abruptly to a stalk at the base.

The fruit is an erect, three-lobed capsule that is three-beaked at the tip. The seeds are whitish or yellowish and number about 10 per section.

This species is restricted to moist or wet prairies in the eastern portion of the tallgrass biome, but when found, it occurs in abundance. Due to its large, conspicuous inflorescence, bunchflower adds a beauty missing from most prairies. It may even act as an indicator species, telling the prairie traveler of wet conditions from a distance.

The rootstock of bunchflower is considered poisonous, but occasionally livestock exhibit poisonous effects after eating its stems and leaves in hay. Symptoms are great muscular weakness, labored breathing, fast heartbeat, and sweating.

The roots have been used to poison flies. Western native Americans used a closely related plant to stun fish.

photograph by Randall A. Maas

Other common names: prairie June grass, crested hair grass, Koeler's grass

Koeleria: in honor of George Ludwig Koeler, a late 18th-century German professor at Mainz and a student of grasses

Cristata: from Latin, meaning "crested"

Grass family: Poaceae (Gramineae)

Found in a wide range of soil conditions throughout the prairies, this species grows in scattered clumps among other species. It does not form pure stands of its own. Flowers late May to July.

Slender, unbranched stems grow 1 to 2 feet tall in the small, close tufts characteristic of bunchgrasses. The root system is fibrous and adaptable to a wide range of soil conditions. Growth and flowering of this cool season perennial is completed in late June, when the grass goes dormant until fall or the following spring.

The plant is leafy at the base. The leaf blades are thin, less than ⅛ inch across, and grow up to 12 inches long. While the leaves are dark green, they are stiff and flat. As they dry, they curl and twist into a spiral shape. They are unevenly veined and rough on the upper surface. Leaf sheaths, at least the lower ones, are usually hairy. These hairs are distinctly curved or bent.

The seed head is a dense, unbranched, spikelike cylinder that tapers toward the tip. It is usually 1 to 6 inches long and ¼ to ½ inch thick. Shiny, silvery green spikelets that are about ¼ inch long crowd together toward the tip of the seed head. There may be space between the spikelets toward the base. June grass is highly variable and tends to have no awns or, if present, only very short ones.

Reproduction is by seeding or transplanting.

While green, June grass is a good forage for deer, elk, and livestock. It becomes less palatable as it matures.

Sometimes it is used as a lawn decoration in areas of open, dry ground. It can also be useful for soil conservation purposes.

In the West, this grass is believed to be one of the plants that cause hay fever during the summer. Anyone planning to use June grass for ornamental or pasture planting should consider this possible reaction to it.

There are about 15 species of *Koeleria* worldwide.

photograph by LeRoy G. Pratt

Other common names: grooved flax

Linum: the classical name for this well-known genus, which includes the species known in ancient times for supplying the fibers for making linen

Sulcatum: meaning "furrowed," from the conspicuous ridges or grooves of the stem

Flax family: Linaceae

Found throughout the tallgrass prairie and elsewhere, especially in dry, sandy soils. Blooms June to July.

This pale green annual has a stiff stem that branches toward the top. Branches have conspicuous grooves or ridges. Yellow flax grows as tall as 30 inches, but most plants are less than 2 feet high. As with other flax species, the stem has a tough, fibrous covering.

The pale green leaves are narrow and usually less than 1 inch long; the margins and both surfaces are smooth. Leaves grow alternately along the stem and are without petioles. Two tiny stipular glands are found where the leaf attaches to the stem.

The five-parted flowers are carried on short (less than ½ inch long) flowerstalks scattered among the branches. The five yellow petals are blunt ovals less than ½ inch long.

Two rows of sepals surround the flower's base. Sepals in the outer row are lance-shaped and about ¼ inch long. Their margins are slightly shorter and more pointed toward the tips than those of the inner row, and their marginal teeth are more prominent. Unlike a similar species, *L. rigidum,* the sepals tend to stay on after the petals drop.

The seeds are flattened crescents. There usually are 10 seeds in each globe-shaped capsule.

Species of flax have been cultivated since before recorded history for the fibers in their stems and the oil in their seeds.

Early settlers were sometimes advised to take 2 tablespoons of flax seed oil twice daily as a treatment for piles. They applied poultices of the powdered seed, cornmeal, and water to wounds and to the enlarged glands of mumps.

American Indians and pioneers sometimes put flax seed in their eyes to help remove foreign matter caught there. They also used flax plant parts for burns and skin ulcers.

Other uses of flax included holding a bag of flax seed against the ear for earache. Flax seed was ground and mixed with ground mustard seed and hog fat or mutton tallow to make a mustard plaster.

A western species with blue flowers is named *L. lewisii* in honor of Meriwether Lewis, the famed explorer. Its seeds were used in cooking and for colds and general debility. Fibers were used for cordage.

Several other species with yellow or blue flowers are also found in the Upper Midwest. *L. rigidum* has a more compact growth habit than *L. sulcatum,* and its branches are not deeply furrowed. It and some other species have been blamed for livestock poisoning because they contain a cyanide compound.

photograph by Sylvan T. Runkel

Other common names: orange cup, orange lily, wild orange lily, tiger lily, huckleberry lily, glade lily, flame lily, wild orange-red lily

Lilium: an ancient classical Latin name for lily, which probably was derived from a still more ancient Greek name

Philadelphicum: meaning "of Philadelphia"

Lily family: Liliaceae

Found throughout the tallgrass prairie and in open woods and thickets east to Maine, south to Kentucky and West Virginia. In spite of its name, the wood lily is often found in the prairie biome, especially the tallgrass prairie region. It prefers the more acid and sandy soils. Additional varieties extend the range to the West Coast. Blooms mid-June to mid-August.

Wood lilies grow 1 to 3 feet high from perennial bulbs. The lanceolate leaves, 1 to 4 inches long and about ¼ to ½ inch wide, are narrowed at both ends. Leaves occur mostly in whorls of three to six sessile leaves. The western wood lily (*L. philadelphicum* var. *andinum*) has top leaves in whorls and lower leaves opposite.

There may be one to three (sometimes five) flowers on each plant. The flower has six sepals, six petals, six stamens, and a three-lobed stigma. Although there is often considerable variation in flower color, it is usually some shade of reddish orange. The color varies from an intense scarlet or deep red to a lighter orange-red or yellow with purple spots on the inside of the flower. Unlike most of the other nodding lily flowers, this one points the 1¼- to 2-inch-long flower upward, which gives rise to one of its common names—orange cup.

The seeds of *Lilium* species are borne in dry capsules with three compartments. Two rows of small seeds are tightly packed in each compartment.

The bulbs have been used for food by various tribes of American Indians. The bulbs of most of the native lilies were cooked and used as foods in various ways; they were boiled, baked, and roasted and also were used for thickening soups.

The roots and leaves of some lilies were applied as poultices to boils and infected sores. A wet dressing of pulverized flowers of the western wood lily was used by the Blackfoot to treat the bite of a "small, brown, poisonous spider."

Some American Indians call this plant mouse root because field mice were known to feed upon the bulbs. In the more northern regions of this lily's habitat, porcupines have also been reported as digging up the bulbs for food.

photograph by LeRoy G. Pratt

Other common names: palespike lobelia, highbelia

Lobelia: named for a 16th century Flemish herbalist, Matthias von Lobel

Spicata: from Latin, meaning "with a spike"

Bluebell or bellflower family: Campanulaceae

Found under a wide range of conditions, from rich meadows to dry, sandy areas, throughout the tallgrass prairies and beyond to the east and south. Blooms June to August.

Single, leafy stems of spiked lobelia are usually unbranched and grow to 3 feet tall from a biennial or perennial rootstock. The stems are usually smooth toward the top but have a covering of short hairs toward the base. At least one variety has a covering of short, stiff hairs.

Light green to bluish green leaves are alternate along the stem. Those toward the base are as long as 3½ inches and sometimes form a basal rosette. Their slender oval shape narrows toward the base to resemble a petiole (leafstalk). The margins are slightly toothed.

This species grows in two forms: one has most leaves on the lower part of the stem and only bracts farther up the stem, the other has leaves scattered along the stem.

The flowers, a pale blue fading to whitish, are arranged in a spike at the top of the stem. Small individual flowers, usually less than ½ inch long, have two distinct lips. The upper lip is divided into two lobes by a cleft that almost extends to its base. The lower lip is deeply cleft into three lobes, each larger than the upper lobes. Five small green sepals surround the base of the flower. A small leaf or bract appears with each flower.

The fruit is short, podlike, and two-celled. Each cell contains many small seeds.

Spiked lobelia has been classified as a diuretic. American Indians and pioneers used various *Lobelia* species for emetic, cathartic, and other purposes. Roots were considered a purgative.

It contains several alkaloids that are similar to nicotine. Animals tend to avoid grazing this plant, but when other plants are dry or in short supply, they may eat enough to be poisoned.

Three closely related species are well known: *L. cardinalis,* the common cardinal flower; *L. siphilitica,* great blue lobelia; and *L. inflata,* Indian tobacco. Although *L. inflata* is called Indian tobacco, it contains a substance that has been used medicinally to cure people of the tobacco smoking habit. It is unlikely that it was used as a smoking tobacco.

photograph by John Schwegman

Other common names: sword grass, lady grass, ladies' lace, bride's lace doggers, spires

Phalaris: from Greek, meaning "shining," alluding to the shining seeds or possibly to the crestlike seed head

Arundinacea: meaning "reedlike"

Grass family: Poaceae (Gramineae)

Found throughout the tallgrass prairie in moist portions and potholes. It grows well in fertile, moist to wet soils and is frequently seen growing in wet, grassed waterways and along pond or stream edges. It also does well on upland soils. Reed canary grass is found throughout the temperate regions of North America as well as in Europe and Asia. Seed heads appear late May to July.

Reed canary grass is a native, cool season, sod-forming perennial grass that grows from 2 to 6 feet in height. As a cool season grass, it generally starts growth earlier in the spring than the warm season grasses and slows its growth during the hot summer months when warm season grasses are growing best. It may add more growth in the cooler fall season. Clumps may reach 2 to 3 feet across, especially where it is growing in thin stands or where it is just establishing itself. It spreads both by seed and creeping rootstock and will gradually fill in between clumps and form a continuous sod cover.

Broad leaves may be 8 inches long and 1 to 2 inches wide. Leaves are usually rough on both sides. The papery ligule is quite prominent and may be 3/16 of an inch long.

The flowers, and later the seed heads, are in tight, dense, cylindrical clusters that may be 6 inches long. These clusters contain many shiny, light tan or brown flax-like seeds in whitish, papery-looking husks that shatter easily.

This plant grows naturally around the Northern Hemisphere; it has been observed in Europe and Asia for many years. It was used in Sweden for planting in wet situations. Although there is a native species, the first seeds for planting in the United States apparently came from Sweden. This grass has probably been planted more than any other for erosion control, pasture, hay, seed, stream edge control, and many other uses in moist to wet to very wet soil situations. However, in some situations it is so aggressive that it has taken over areas where it was not wanted. As a member of the early tallgrass prairie, it seems to have been environmentally suited to its original location.

A variety of *Phalaris* called ribbon grass (*P. arundinacea* var. *picta*), which has leaf blades streaked with white, has been planted ornamentally. Sometimes it escapes from cultivation. This variety is also called gardener's garters.

photograph by Ted Van Bruggen

Other common names: flat-topped spurge, milk purslane, milkweed, snake milk, tramp's spurge, white-flowered milkweed, wild hippo

Euphorbia: probably named for Euphorbus, a physician to King Juba of Numidia, an ancient country in an area of northern Africa that more or less corresponds to the present Algeria

Corollata: from Latin, meaning "with corollas"

Spurge family: Euphorbiaceae

Found on dry soils, often in open clearings, old pastures, dry pastures, and roadsides, throughout the tallgrass prairie and to the east and the south. Blooms from June to October.

The one or more bright green stems of flowering spurge grow erect, up to 3 feet tall, from tough, stout, deep, perennial roots. The stem is usually smooth, rarely softly hairy. Distinct spots may appear on the stems.

The leaves are scattered alternately along the lower stem. They are slender ovals less than 2 inches long. The margins are smooth, and petioles are absent or quite short. (The milky juice of the foliage is irritating, and it may cause blistering if left on the skin.)

A whorl of leaves (one leaf for each flowerstalk) surrounds the stem at the point where three to seven slender flowerstalks branch off. Each flowerstalk branches again above another whorl of smaller leaves.

Flowerstalks tipped with small white "flowers" form a loose, flat-topped flower head that may be as much as 8 inches across. Each "flower" has five conspicuous, white, egg-shaped, petal-like bracts that form a cuplike base for the true flowers, which are greenish in color and perhaps $1/12$ inch high. The cuplike base may be $1/4$ to $1/2$ inch across.

The fruit is a three-celled capsule with one seed in each section. The egg-shaped seeds are less than $1/8$ inch across and vary from light brown to mottled gray. A dark line (or point of attachment) marks one side of the seed.

Flowering spurge was a favorite of American Indians. They used it in combination with juices of other plants to dissolve warts and similar growths on the skin. Combined with other plants, it served the Meskwaki as a laxative and a cathartic and a treatment for rheumatism and pin worms. The powdered bark of its roots was widely used as a purgative.

Although an overdose was dangerous, the powdered root bark was popular during the 19th century as an emetic, a diaphoretic, an expectorant, and an epispastic. In spite of its irritating and potentially poisonous side effects, it was once considered to be among the best of remedies for dropsy. Similar use of this plant in earlier times gave rise to the common name spurge, which is from the Latin *expurgare,* meaning "to purge."

This poisonous plant is seldom eaten by livestock. It is, however, an important part of the prairie chicken diet.

Two close relatives are *E. marginata,* snow-on-the-mountain, and *E. pulcherrima,* the popular Christmas poinsettia.

photograph by Linda Gucciardo

Other common names: blue stem wheat grass

Agropyron: from the Greek *agrios,* meaning "wild," and *pyros,* meaning "wheat"

Smithii: named in honor of Jared Gage Smith

Grass family: Poaceae (Gramineae)

Found in fine-textured soils of low areas where runoff water accumulates, often in nearly pure stands. It is most common in mixed prairies of the Great Plains. It is found in scattered locations eastward to the edge of the deciduous woodland. Western wheat grass makes its maximum growth in the spring; it flowers and produces seed in June.

Western wheat grass is a drought-tolerant, sod-forming, cool season perennial that generally grows 2 to 3 feet tall. The stems stand stiffly erect.

The leaf blades, mostly 4 to 12 inches long and less than ¼ inch wide, tend to be stiff and erect despite their length. Flat and firm when green, the leaves are curled to the point of looking wirelike when dry. They are strongly ribbed on the upper surface and feel rough to the touch.

Both leaves and stems have a whitish bloom that tends to make them appear blue-green. Logically, this is the basis for the somewhat descriptive name of blue stem wheat grass.

The dense, fibrous root system includes long, branching, scaly, tawny-colored rhizomes.

The tight, erect grainlike seed head is 4 to 6 inches long. Spikelets are usually borne singly at joints of the seed stalk. Seldom occurring in pairs, they generally alternate along the stalk, resulting in a somewhat flattened head. Space between the spikelets varies; the spikelets range from being crowded to having enough space between them to give the head an irregular lobed appearance. Variation may occur within a single head. The 9 to 13 flowers within each spikelet are crowded together to make the spikelet quite dense.

Awns, if present, are quite short. The seeds are relatively large for grasses, requiring 100,000 to 125,000 per pound.

This species provides good pasturage except during its midsummer dormancy. Western wheat grass is especially good during winter because the foliage starts to grow in the fall and tends to remain green during the winter. Its sod-forming ability and water tolerance make it useful for erosion control.

A close relative is the common and pesky quackgrass (*A. repens*), an immigrant from Europe. Early settlers used the quackgrass root for its diuretic and laxative properties. During times of great scarcity, they ground the roots for meal to make bread. The root also was the source of a gray dye.

A third species, *A. desertorum,* is found only in extreme xeric habitats in the western part of the region.

Birds and small mammals use plants of this genus as cover; grazing animals use them as food.

Western wheat grass is one of the few grasses honored by a state. In 1970 South Dakota chose it for the state grass.

photograph by Ted Van Bruggen

Other common names: beaver poison, cowbane, musquash root, spotted cowbane, spotted hemlock

Cicuta: the ancient Latin name for poison hemlock

Maculata: from Latin, meaning "spotted" or "mottled"

Parsley family: Apiaceae (Umbelliferae)

Found in low, wet, swampy prairies and open areas to the east of the Great Plains, preferring wetter areas than poison hemlock, *Conium maculatum.* Blooms June through August.

The stoutish stem of this biennial, or short-lived perennial, grows to 7 feet tall. It is erect, with slender branches. The lower part is often lined or mottled with purple, as is the stem of poison hemlock. The thickened base of the stem is hollow but has distinct cross sections.

Fleshy tubers cluster finger-like at the base of the stem. Despite resembling small sweet potatoes and having a fragrance like that of parsnips, these roots are poisonous. When cut crosswise, the roots exude an aromatic, yellow oil.

The dark green pinnately compound leaves have fewer and coarser leaflets than poison hemlock. The larger lower leaves are about 1 foot long and are on long petioles; they are generally tipped with three leaflets. Other units of leaflets along the central petiole may have one or two leaflets. Leaflets are narrow and lance-shaped, not finely cut like those of poison hemlock. Midribs and veins are prominent on the underside. The veins end in the notches of the leaflet margins.

The flat-topped flower heads, 2 to 5 inches across, are made up of several smaller heads. Individual flowers are tiny, about 1/16 inch across, and have a slight fragrance.

The oval fruits, which have alternating rounded ribs and dark furrows, are about 1/8 inch long.

Though very poisonous, water hemlock is less toxic than poison hemlock. (Poisoning from poison hemlock seeds is always fatal, but if given soon enough, treatment for poisoning from water hemlock roots is sometimes effective.) One of the chief symptoms of poisoning from water hemlock is severe convulsions, whereas that from poison hemlock is respiratory paralysis.

A poisonous resin, cicuta toxin, is concentrated in the elongate tubers at the base of the stem. If ingested, a piece of tuber the size of a pea is sufficient to cause death in humans. If eaten in spring when the toxin is most concentrated, a piece of root the size of a walnut can kill a cow.

A volatile alkaloid, cicutine, can be extracted from the oil of the root. When properly used, it is helpful in relieving epilepsy, convulsions, and psychoses. Although prescribed for sick and nervous headaches in the past, it is seldom used now.

The Klamath Indians prepared a mixture of rotted deer liver, rattlesnake venom, and the juice of water hemlock and used it as a poison on the tips of arrows.

The Cherokee thought water hemlock could be used as an oral contraceptive. Occasionally, the roots were used in an attempt to induce permanent sterility, but this was a dangerous procedure—one that could be fatal.

photograph by Tomma Lou Maas

Poison hemlock: *Conium maculatum* L.

Other common names: snakeweed, St. Bennet's–herb, poison parsley, wode-whistle, spotted parsley, bunk

Conium: from the Greek *coneion,* name of the hemlock by which Socrates was put to death in ancient Athens

Maculatum: from Latin, meaning "spotted" or "mottled"

Parsley family: Apiaceae (Umbelliferae)

Found in moist places, especially waste ground, throughout the country, preferring drier areas than does water hemlock, *Cicuta maculata*. Flowers June and July.

This introduced biennial grows 5 feet or more tall from a whitish, carrot-shaped taproot. The stout, hollow, much-branched stem is smooth and a pale green with reddish or purple spots.

The pinnately compound leaves are deeply cut and finely dissected, appearing fernlike. The overall leaf is rather triangular with bluntly rounded corners. The individual leaflets are smaller ovals. The lower leaves have long petioles, while the upper ones have short petioles or none at all. When bruised, the leaves and stems give off a fetid odor.

The tiny white flowers, less than 1/10 inch across, are borne in groups of small heads. Each of these small heads is carried on a short stalk that arises from a common point on the main flowerstalk. Together, they make up a larger flower head. The loose arrangement of such flower heads makes the top of a poison hemlock plant white. Close examination of the tiny flowers shows fine, white petals but no sepals.

The fruits are a pair of nutlets that are more or less flattened ovals with winged margins. Most of the seed surface is covered with fine, prominent ribs. The unribbed surface is concave. These small seeds are about 1/10 inch across. Without close examination, the seeds may easily be mistaken for anise seeds, which produce the oil of anise used in the confectionery business.

This plant, especially the seed, is highly poisonous. It contains the toxic volatile alkaloid coniine and other toxins, such as conhydrine and methylconiine. Supposedly ancient Greeks used it to provide a quick death in the disposal of prisoners.

Poison hemlock has been used as a medicinal herb since ancient times. Because of their fear of rabies, people mixed it with wine and drank the mixture for the "bite of the mad dogge." As a last resort, it was administered as an antidote for strychnine and other virulent poisons. It was more safely used externally as a poultice for tumors, ulcers, pains of joints, and scrofulous infections. In the 15th and 16th centuries, some tried it as a cure for cancerous ulcers.

The leaves and unripe fruits of poison hemlock were used medicinally as sedatives, as anodynes (pain relievers), and as antispasmodics for stomach pains and for such illnesses as asthma, epilepsy, whooping cough, angina, and cholera. Overdoses caused paralysis, so it was used with extreme caution.

Follow the recommendation of "knowing and not nibbling" plants of this family!

photograph by Sylvan T. Runkel

Other common names: tickseed, stiff tickseed, stiff coreopsis

Coreopsis: from the Greek, meaning "having the appearance of a bug," referring to the buglike shape of the seeds. The common name tickseed also refers to the ticklike shape of the seed.

Palmata: means "palmate," like the fingers radiating out from the hand or "palm," referring to the shape of the leaves

Daisy family: Asteraceae (Compositae)

This native plant is found throughout the Upper Midwest, mostly on prairies. Blooms June through July.

This perennial grows to be 1 to 3 feet high. Many alternate, simple leaves, each 2 to 3 inches long, grow along the stiff stem. The stiff leaves are sessile. Each leaf has three long, narrow lobes, giving it the appearance of a crow's foot.

The rootstock is horizontal.

Each plant has relatively few bright yellow flower heads, each 1 to 2 inches across. Rays (like petals) are 6 to 10 in number, and each one is generally tipped with three teeth.

The seeds, or achenes, are about 1/10 inch long.

This species was used by the Meskwaki, who boiled the seeds and drank the brew. Some tribes made a poultice of the boiled seeds and put it on painful areas of the body to relieve ailments such as rheumatism.

Some species, especially *C. tinctoria,* were used as dye plants.

Beekeepers consider *Coreopsis* species to be good sources of honey.

The genus *Coreopsis* is an important component of the tall-grass biome; at least five species occur there. Related species are *C. tinctoria,* an annual with opposite leaves, the lower of which are pinnately divided, and with red or purplish ray flowers; *C. grandiflora,* with large yellow flowers; *C. lanceolata,* with leaves mostly at the base of the stem; and *C. tripteris,* with leaves divided into three to five elliptic leaflets. Tall coreopsis, *C. tripteris,* and lance-leaved tickseed, *C. lanceolata,* are native to the Upper Midwest.

Several garden flowers have been derived from wildflowers of this genus: *C. grandiflora* and *C. tinctoria* are showy examples.

photograph by Richard F. Trump

Other common names: wild pea, locoweed

Crotalaria: from the Greek *crotalon,* meaning a "rattle," in reference to the loose seeds inside the inflated pod

Sagittalis: from Latin, meaning "like an arrowhead," for the shape of the stipules of the upper leaves

Legume family: Fabaceae (Leguminosae)

Found in dry, sandy, or gravelly soils of prairies and other open areas. Blooms from June through September.

This annual legume grows to 16 inches tall. The stems may be simple or branched, erect or partially reclining. They are covered with fine hairs that are spreading or pointed upward along the stem.

Leaves are alternate and simple, with a short petiole. Lower leaves are oval in shape, tapering toward the base and tip; upper leaves are narrower. The larger leaves are 1 to 1½ inches long and ⅙ to ⅔ inch across. The upper leaves have distinctive and conspicuous stipules shaped as arrowheads pointing downward; these may occur on lower leaves also. (This is the basis of the species name.) The stipule is a bractlike, persistent appendage on the stem at the base of the leaves.

Elongated clusters of two to four flowers appear on 1- to 4-inch-long stalks that arise from the axils of the upper leaves. The yellow, pea-like flowers are on short individual stalks that are perhaps ¼ inch long. The flower is divided into a two-lobed upper lip and a three-lobed lower lip. A circle of green floral leaves is at the base of each flower. These leaves are slightly hairy and about as long as the flower itself, sometimes slightly longer.

Seeds are carried in an inflated, smooth, blackish pod about 1 inch long and ⅓ inch wide. The pods contain two to several shiny, kidney-shaped seeds that become loose at maturity.

The small, pea-like seeds of rattlebox have been used as a substitute for coffee. Ground seeds may be toxic to pigs and be a purge to cattle. Roasting may get rid of the toxic property, however.

Rattlebox caused mortality in horses pastured in localized parts of the Missouri River valley in the 1880s. Death was often slow, taking 10 days to several weeks. Horses in upland pastures seemed immune to this so-called bottom disease. Although important for only a few years, it caused an extensive loss of horses during that time. Cattle seem to be immune.

In warmer climates, some introduced species have become important cover crops, especially in orange groves, where they supply nitrogen. Blooming in early winter, they become a source of baking-quality honey. The flavor is not good enough for table honey.

In warmer climates, some species are cultivated as ornamentals.

photograph by Ted Van Bruggen

Other common names: pleurisy root, butterfly weed, yellow milkweed, orange swallowwort, orangeroot, whiteroot, Indian posy, windroot, Canada tuber, Canada flux, chigger flower

Asclepias: from the name of the Greek god of healing and medicine

Tuberosa: meaning "tuberous," referring to the tuberous root

Milkweed family: Asclepiadaceae

Found throughout the tallgrass biome in dry, open areas, usually in prairies or prairie relicts. Occasionally it is found along old country roads or old or abandoned roads or railroad rights-of-way. Flowers from June to September.

The stout, simple or terminally branched stems are generally clumped and may be up to 2½ feet high. Rough-pointed leaves up to 6 inches long alternate along the stem. The typical milkweed milky sap is lacking; instead, a watery juice exudes from the cut stem.

The flowers are normally bright orange but occasionally are yellow. Many individual flowers are in a head.

The flowers attract insects, but like the flowers of other milkweed plants, they are designed to favor larger flying pollinators and to prevent crawling insects from getting to the nectar. As with other milkweeds, only a few of the numerous flowers get pollinated, so ordinarily a plant has only one or two pods. This is due to a complex pollinating mechanism where the pollen sacs are attached to a structure located in the slit between the anthers.

This pollinium, which sticks to the pollinating insect, must be pulled free and carried to another flower. Many insects lack the strength to pull this structure or themselves free and are found dead on the flower head.

The spindle-shaped pods, 3 to 5 inches long, contain many seeds. Each seed has a silky plume to aid in its dispersal.

This species reproduces by seed and by rootstock. It is easily established in gardens or in restored prairies from seed, but transplanting is difficult because the root is stout and deep.

At one time this root was considered to be a cure for pleurisy, hence, the name pleurisy root. Early doctors listed pleurisy root as a subtonic, diaphoretic, alterative, expectorant, diuretic, laxative, escharotic, carminative, astringent, antirheumatic, and antisyphilitic.

The root is enlarged. This gave rise to the last part of the scientific name.

Butterfly milkweed is one of the most striking species of the tallgrass biome. The bright color may attract insects, including butterflies, hence, its common name.

At least 16 species of milkweed occur in the heart of the tallgrass prairie. Some provide an index of prairie quality; none are as showy as the butterfly milkweed.

photograph by John Schwegman

Other common names: button snakeroot, yucca-leaf eryngo, corn snakeroot, water-eryngo, rattlesnake flag, rattlesnake weed

Eryngium: from the Greek for "a prickly plant," referring to the apparent prickle-like leaves of this plant (although they are neither prickly nor sharp)

Yuccifolium: from the Greek for "yucca leaves," referring to the yuccalike appearance of the leaves

Parsley family: Apiaceae (Umbelliferae)

Found generally on wet or dry prairies and prairie relicts throughout the Upper Midwest. Blooms June to September.

This stout perennial grows 2 to 6 feet high from a short, thick rootstock. The bluish green basal leaves are up to 3 feet long and up to 1½ inches wide. The leaves along the stem are much shorter, but they may be as wide as the basal leaves. All of the leaves are thick and parallel veined and have soft or weak prickles along the edges. The bristles are spaced far apart. The leaf bases clasp the single, erect stem.

There are several flower heads on stout peduncles at the tip of the stem. Each globose or nearly spherical flower head is from ½ to 1 inch in diameter. Each head is made up of many small flowers. Whitish bracts stick out sharply from the flowers, which gives the flower head a rough, prickly feel and appearance. The heads have a "honeylike" odor.

Individual fruits, which mature in the spherical flower head, are less than ¹⁄₁₀ inch long.

The root of rattlesnake master has been used medicinally by American Indians and pioneers. It served as a diaphoretic, expectorant, and emetic in early medicine in the United States. The root also has been used to treat liver troubles.

The Meskwaki used *E. yuccifolium* as a diuretic and as a medicine for bladder troubles and for poisons other than rattlesnake venom. Chewing the root induced a flow of saliva. Roots mashed in cold water made a drink for relieving muscular pains.

From the root of a similar species, the Creeks made a drink they took to induce vomiting before they went hunting or attended ceremonies. The same species was used to treat neuralgia, kidney trouble, snakebite, and rheumatism.

Among the early uses of rattlesnake master reported by C. F. Millspaugh was that of a tea of the boiled root to treat "exhaustion from sexual depletion." A related plant was mentioned in Shakespeare's *Merry Wives of Windsor*. One author reported a related species was regarded as an "aphrodisiac exciting venereal desires" and a "strengthener of procreative organs." Candied root generally was used for these purposes. It was also recommended for treating hemorrhoids, venereal diseases, and bites of insects or snakes.

Even the ancient Greeks used plants of this genus for medicinal purposes.

At least two or three other species of *Eryngium* are found in different parts of the United States.

photograph by Richard F. Trump

Other common names: meadow sweet

Filipendula: from Latin *filum* for "thread" and *pendulus* for "hanging," in reference to the small tubers strung together by the fibrous roots of one species

Rubra: from Latin, meaning "red"

Rose family: Rosaceae

Found in moist prairies and open places, mostly to the east of the Great Plains. Blooming time is June through July.

Queen-of-the-prairie is a tall, regal plant deserving of its common name. Its softly hairy, branched stem grows 2 to 8 feet tall, towering above most other prairie plants. The plant spreads by perennial rhizomes.

The large, alternate leaves, on petioles, may be up to 3 feet long. All leaflets except the terminal one are placed opposite along the main petiole. The end leaflet is larger than the others and deeply cut into seven or nine lobes. The lateral leaflets, without their own petioles, may be deeply cut into as many as five lobes. The lobes run evenly and are coarsely toothed.

The spectacular blooms of queen-of-the-prairie also ensure that the plant deserves its name. The flowers are grouped into large, feathery clusters that may be from 4 to nearly 10 inches across and up to more than 12 inches long. Individual flowers are small, about ½ inch across, but the five petals are a deep peach to pink color. Petals are narrowed at their bases. Numerous sta-

mens give the flowers a somewhat fluffy appearance.

The fruit is a dry, indehiscent, one-seeded capsule.

Queen-of-the-prairie contains salicylic acid, which has antiseptic properties. Since it has mild analgesic properties, it resembles the action as well as the chemistry of aspirin. This plant has been used for influenza, gout, rheumatism, arthritis, and fever. Other conditions treated with it were diarrhea, dropsy, water retention, and bladder and kidney ailments. It also provided a wash for wounds.

Due to its tannin content, queen-of-the-prairie has astringent properties. Therefore, many Plains Indians sought the plant for treating skin rashes and diseases.

Used as a treatment for heart trouble, the root was also an ingredient in love potions. (In the references, it is difficult to separate the physical from the emotional aspects of these uses.)

Meadow queen (*F. ulmaria*), a related species introduced from Europe and Asia, is found in more eastern states. It is a shorter plant with white or greenish flowers. It was once used to flavor a fermented beverage called mead.

photograph by Kitty Kohout

Other common names: meadow rose, prairie rose

Rosa: from ancient Latin, the name for "rose"

Species: Several species occur frequently on the tallgrass prairie.

Rose family: Rosaceae

Found throughout the tallgrass biome in a wide range of habitats, from open woodlands to roadsides to disturbed areas to native prairies. Blooms June through late summer.

Normally the wild rose is a woody shrub that grows up to 4 feet in height. Older stems are branched, and prickles are present in varying numbers. Some species, such as *R. blanda,* have few prickles.

The spreading, perennial root system often sends up new shoots.

Leaves are generally divided into five to seven leaflets that are arranged in opposite pairs except for the solitary terminal leaflet. The leaflets are sharply toothed ovals, normally less than 1½ inches long.

Solitary or in clusters of a few, flowers usually appear on the new growth branching from older stems. The showy flowers are large, up to 2 inches across; they have five broad petals that sometimes are shallowly notched. Petals, in varying shades of pink, are set off by numerous yellow stamens. Five green sepals join to form an urn-shaped base for the flower.

This base matures into a smooth, red, apple-like fruit ½ inch in diameter. These fruits, or hips, maintain their color into winter.

The Meskawki and the Menomini boiled the hips to make a syrup for various nutritional uses. Skins of hips were used for stomach troubles. The Chippewa scraped the second layer of root bark onto a cloth, soaked it in water, and squeezed drops of the liquid into sore eyes. This was followed by a similar preparation from red raspberry root. Mescalero Apaches boiled rosebuds and drank the liquid as a treatment for gonorrhea.

Native Americans and pioneers ate the hips, flowers, leaves, and new shoots when other food was scarce. Rose hips are still an important wildlife food.

Three rose hips are said to contain as much vitamin C as an orange. Health food stores often sell rose hips.

The rose has been cultivated as a garden plant for over 2000 years. Ancient Greeks and later the Romans used roses in garlands and at social affairs.

The climbing roses now popular in cultivated gardens are descendants of native wild roses.

photograph by Sylvan T. Runkel

Other common names: brown Betty, brown daisy, brown-eyed Susan, coneflower, donkeybead, English bull's eye, poor-land daisy, yellow daisy, yellow Jerusalem, yellow ox-eye daisy, deer eye (Cherokee)

Rudbeckia: named in honor of two Rudbecks, father and son botanists, who preceded Linnaeus at the University in Upsala, Sweden

Serotina: from Latin *serum,* meaning "late"

Daisy family: Asteraceae (Compositae)

Found throughout the tallgrass prairie and elsewhere under a wide variety of environments but generally preferring drier areas. Blooms from June to September.

This short-lived perennial grows erect to 3 feet tall. Its stem, usually without branches below the flower head, is rough and hairy.

Basal leaves up to 5 inches long and 1 inch across are often broadest toward their tips. Along the stem, leaves are alternate, smaller, and have no petiole. Leaves tend to be thick, rough, and hairy; they may be finely toothed on the margin.

The bright orange-yellow flowers, one or a few per stem, have 10 to 20 ray petals that are perhaps an inch long. These petals are arranged around a dome-shaped center disk. This dark brown disk is usually ½ to ¾ inch across. Flowers are carried on individual stalks that may be long or short.

The seed is a tiny, four-angled achene.

Early settlers used black-eyed Susan as a stimulant and a diuretic. Leaves were dried and steeped to brew a tea considered by these settlers to be a kidney stimulant. A drink made by steeping the leaves of another species, *R. hirta,* was also used as a kidney stimulant.

The Forest Potawatomi prepared a root tea of this or other species for curing colds. A related species, *R. laciniata,* was used as a diuretic and a tonic. The disk flowers were boiled with rushes to give them a yellow color.

Other species of the genus have been widely used as garden ornamentals, especially in Europe. Golden glow is a *Rudbeckia* that was widely planted in flower gardens in the past.

Because black-eyed Susan is sometimes found growing in hayfields and pastures, some people class it as a weed. It is easily controlled, however, and it adds a touch of beauty to prairie, roadside, or meadow.

photograph by Sylvan T. Runkel

Other common names: bigtop dalea, plume dalea, slender parosela

Dalea: once called *Parosela;* renamed after Samuel Dale, an early English botanist

Enneandra: from Latin, meaning "with nine stamens"

Legume family: Fabaceae (Leguminosae)

Found on dry ridgetops and hillsides throughout the western parts of the tallgrass prairie, this species is a fragile-looking member of the flora. It blooms from late May into August.

The slender, reddish stems of nine-anther dalea grow up to 4 feet tall. The stems branch above the middle of the plant, and these branches terminate in flowering spikes. The stems are smooth and have glandular spots.

Small, pinnate leaves alternate along the stem. Each leaf has two to five pairs of opposite leaflets and one leaflet at the tip of the central vein. The leaflets, about ¼ inch long, are ovals that are narrower toward the base.

The woody, perennial taproot is yellow, but it turns orange after exposure to sunlight and air.

The flowers occur in loose spikes that may be 5 inches long. There is space between each flower on the spike. Individual flowers have conspicuous and persistent bracts. The bracts are broad ovals about ⅛ inch long that generally have a rather blunt tip. The white, pea-like flowers are only about ½ inch long. The upper petal (the standard) is smaller than the other petals and is heart-shaped. The side petals (wings) are shorter than the bottom petal or keel. The green, caplike calyx, which surrounds the petals, has long teeth that are fringed with hairs.

The fruit is a membranous pod containing a single seed.

The Plains Indians crushed the leaves of a relative, *D. aurea,* to prepare a drink to treat colic and dysentery. The Hopi ate the roots of another relative, *D. terminalis,* and ground its seeds into a flour.

Honey made from the plants of this genus is of splendid quality.

Another dalea, foxtail dalea (*D. alopecuroides,* also called *D. leporina*), occurs in the western portion of the tallgrass biome. An annual with 19 to 35 leaflets, it occupies a greater variety of habitats than *D. enneandra,* including alluvial open ground and borders or oxbows.

Silktop dalea (*D. aurea*), with golden petals, occurs in the northern Great Plains.

All of these daleas are sparsely distributed over the prairie landscape, and they do not occur in dense stands.

photograph by Ted Van Bruggen

Other common names: hairy ruellia

Ruellia: in honor of an early French herbalist, Jean de la Ruelle (1474–1537)

Humilis: from Latin, meaning "low," in reference to the low-growing habit of the species in many habitats. (Due to variance in the genus, some authorities combine this species with another species, *R. carolinensis.*)

Acanthus family: Acanthaceae

Found throughout the western part of the tallgrass prairie region in a variety of habitats, from open woodlands to moist prairies to sand plains. Blooms from June to August.

The stout, multibranched stem of wild petunia may achieve a height of over 2 feet but is normally less than a foot tall. Depending on the habitat, it may be so low-growing as to appear as a ground cover. One or several stems arise from a perennial, fibrous root system. The short internodes give the plant a short, bushy, leafy appearance. The stem and branches are conspicuously hairy.

The opposite leaves are pointed ovals, usually less than 3 inches long, with those in the middle being slightly longer. There may be up to 12 pairs of leaves along the stem. Leaf margins are smooth, and the whole leaf has a leathery texture and a conspicuous hairy nature, especially along the veins and margins. Leaves are without petioles (sessile) or with very short petioles.

The showy flowers are petunia-shaped and vary from light lavender to purple. They are smaller and not as widely flared as the common cultivated petunia (which belongs to another plant family, the Solonaceae). The corolla has five shallow lobes and is fused into a tube. The corolla may be up to 3 inches long but is usually less. The flowers arise without peduncles from the axils of the upper leaves. A few flowers remain unopened and budlike and are self-fertilized.

The fruit is a dry, oval capsule less than an inch long. It contains several small, round seeds. The calyx, which surrounds the capsule, has five segments that are quite hairy and protrude beyond the capsule.

Although a fairly common and widespread member of the prairie flora, wild petunia does not seem to have been used for medicinal uses by native Americans or settlers.

Although members of this family are mainly confined to tropical areas of the Western Hemisphere, the leaves of a Mediterranean *Acanthus* species may have been the inspiration for the design at the top of ancient Greek Corinthian columns.

photograph by LeRoy G. Pratt

Other common names: narrow-leaved meadow sweet

Spiraea: the ancient Greek name; from *spiraea,* meaning generally "a wreath spiraled or twisted," for the twisted seedpods of some species

Alba: from Latin, meaning "white"

Rose family: Rosaceae

Found in low, wet prairies and other moist, open areas, mostly in the northeastern quarter of the United States and in parts of Canada. Blooms from June to August.

This low-growing, shrubby perennial is generally less than 3 feet tall, but it may reach a height of 6 feet. A few tough, slender stems arise from a more or less running rootstock. The twigs are a dull brown to yellowish brown and may be covered with fine hairs.

The dark green leaves have short petioles and are alternate along the stem. They are shaped as long, pointed ovals. The firm- textured, feather-veined, smooth leaves are finely toothed on the margins. Leaves may be 1 to 2 inches or more long and are about one-third as wide.

The flower head, a branching cluster 2 to 8 inches long, is not as wide as it is long. This rather large head is made up of numerous tiny white flowers, each probably less than ⅛ inch across. Close examination shows five separate, slightly rounded petals on a tiny, green, bell-shaped base that usually has fine, distinct lobes.

The fruit is a dry capsule containing a few long, narrow seeds that are tapered toward the ends.

This plant had wide use in prehistoric and early settlement times. Early settlers valued the root of meadow sweet as food and for a tonic. They used the herbage as an astringent and a diuretic. The inner bark was used as an aspirin substitute. When trapping, the Ojibwa used the root as an animal attractant, and they used the flowers and leaves to prepare a tea to ease childbirth. The Forest Potawatomi considered the bark to have medicinal value. The Meskwaki used immature seeds to prepare a medicine to stop the bloody flux.

A related species, *S. tomentosa,* also has a rich medicinal history. The leaves and bark were used to produce a tea for treating diarrhea. A poultice of the leaves and bark was used to treat tumors and ulcers. It was recognized as an astringent in the late 1800s.

About 70 species of *Spiraea* are native to the United States. Recently, several species have been used in landscaping.

photograph by Randall A. Maas

Other common names: maid-of-the-mist, purple meadow rue

Thalictrum: the name of a plant mentioned by Dioscorides, an ancient Greek naturalist, and later applied to this genus

Dasycarpum: from Latin, meaning "hairy-carpelled." (A carpel is the seed-bearing organ of the plant or a unit of that organ.)

Buttercup family: Ranunculaceae

Found in moist to wet prairies and meadows and along streambanks. Blooms June through July.

A, fibrous, leafy stem grows erect to heights of 6 feet or more from a perennial rootstock. The stem, which frequently has a purplish tinge, is branched toward the top.

Leaves along the stem are alternate and at least the upper ones are without petioles. The basal leaves form a rounded clump. Both basal and stem leaves are divided into three segments that are are often further subdivided into leaflets, each with its own stalk. Leaflets are dark green above, paler with strong veins beneath. The underside is often covered with tiny hairs. These leaflets have three main pointed lobes, all near the tip.

Masses of soft, feathery flowers tower above surrounding growth. The multibranched flower heads are often a foot or more in length. Each flower is borne on its own slender stalk. This flower has no true petals. The four or five greenish, petal-like sepals are shaped like narrow ovals with slender tips.

A distinctive feature of the male flower, which is more fluffy and delicate than the female flower, is the mass of long, conspicuous, whitish stamens that may have a purplish or brownish tinge. Female flowers are dull and coarse in appearance. Male and female flowers are usually on separate plants, but occasionally both kinds of flowers are found on the same plant.

Seeds, perhaps ¼ inch long and about ¹⁄₁₂ inch across, are narrow and somewhat pointed ovals. Each has distinctive ribs or grooves. Each flower generally produces 4 to 15 seeds.

The Ojibwa used the root of meadow rue to make a tea for reducing fevers. They also used it as a tonic, a stimulant, and an antiperiodic.

The Forest Potawatomi smoked the seeds for good luck while hunting. Young men of the tribe would smoke a mixture of these seeds and tobacco when calling on a special lady friend.

The seeds of *T. dasycarpum* are the best source of a drug called thalicarpine, which is believed to be a possible cancer control. The drug has been used successfully with rats; research is continuing with humans.

Because of its conspicuous, large, feathery flower heads, meadow rue is sometimes planted in flower gardens, where it usually grows very well. It will grow in any good, well-drained, loamy soil.

There are 80 to 90 species in this genus; most are found in the temperate zone, but some are found in the tropics. Most of the early-flowering species of the genus grow in woodlands, while the later-flowering species are more often found in moist areas of open prairie swales.

photograph by Tomma Lou Maas

Other common names: blue jackets, cow slobbers, Job's tears, Ohio spiderwort, widow tears

Tradescantia: in honor of John (the older) Tradescant, gardener to Charles I, King of England in the early 17th century

Ohiensis: meaning "of or from Ohio"

Spiderwort family: Commelinaceae

Found in a wide range of environments throughout the prairies, especially in the tallgrass prairie region and to the east and south. Blooms June through August.

The erect, slender stem of this colorful perennial is often branched. It may be green or have a purplish tinge. A distinctive whitish bloom gives it the appearance of having been dusted with fine powder. It usually has three to eight nodes and may be 30 inches tall. The sap is thick, resembling mucilage.

The leaves are alternate and somewhat grasslike, generally ⅕ inch to nearly 2 inches across and perhaps 18 inches long. They are firm and smooth, with a distinctive keel-like midrib. The sheath, which may be covered with fine hairs, is usually 5 to 15 inches long, much longer than the internodes.

Dense, showy clusters of blue or purple (sometimes rose or white) flowers appear at the top of the stem. Each flower has three oval petals from ¼ to ¾ inch long and six golden stamens. The flower is ¾ to more than 1 inch across. Below the petals are three green leaflike sepals that are oval in shape, but their margins tend to be curled inward. Two long, unequal bracts occur beneath the flower cluster.

The flowers tend to open in the morning. When touched in the heat of the day, they shrivel to a fluid jelly that trickles like a tear, which accounts for several common names.

The fruit is a three-celled, generally oval capsule about ¼ inch long. It usually contains three or six seeds.

The plant was once thought to be a cure for spider bites, hence, the common name spiderwort. American Indians used the stems of several species as pot herbs.

It is used in biology classes to study the movement of protoplasm in the hairs in the center of the flower.

Because some selected plants have been found to change flower color when exposed to nuclear or radioactive radiation, the spiderwort has recently been adopted by some environmental and activist groups as a plant watchdog or indicator of radiation or nuclear activity in areas around nuclear plants.

In *Uses of Plants by the Indians of the Missouri River Region,* Melvin Gilmore wrote: "When a young Dakota brave is in love and when walking alone in the prairie and finding this flower in bloom, he sings a song to it in which he endows it with his sweetheart's characteristics and beauty." Part of the song may be translated as:

> Wee little dewy flower
> So blessed and so shy
> You're dear to me, and
> For my love for thee, I'd die

photograph by Randall A. Maas

Other common names: alkali grass, smooth camass, white camass

Zigadenus (also *Zygadenus*): probably from Greek *zygos,* meaning "a yoke," and *aden,* meaning "a gland," because the glands sometimes occur in pairs. (Also called *Anticlea.*)

Elegans: from Latin for "elegant," perhaps in reference to the showy flower heads

Lily family: Liliaceae

Found in prairies and open, rocky areas, especially with high-lime soils, mostly west of the Mississippi River. Blooms in June and July.

This perennial is a pale green color that looks as if it has been dulled by a dusting of white powder. It grows to 3 feet tall from an elongated bulb, the outer coats of which are fibrous. The pale green, grasslike leaves, up to 12 inches long and ½ inch wide, are mainly basal. The smaller stem leaves sheath the stem. The underside has a protruding midrib.

A slender cylinder of showy flowers makes death camas a conspicuous lilylike raceme. The flower head may be 12 inches or more long. Individual flowers on short slender stalks are yellowish or greenish white—sometimes described as "dirty." They are usually less than 1 inch across. Three petals and three similar sepals are narrow-pointed ovals; they produce a flower faintly resembling a star. The center has six prominent stamens (male flower parts) that are about as long as the petals. The inner edge of the base of the petals and sepals is powdery yellow. Beneath each flower are rather large green or purplish bracts.

The fruit is a three-angled, somewhat egg-shaped capsule about ¾ inch long. Each of the three segments ends in a pointed beak. The numerous seeds are ½ inch long.

American Indians were aware of the poisonous nature of the plant, but once in a while they mistook the bulbs for others that are edible. Although odorless and tasteless, the leaves and bulb of death camas are easily confused with those of the harmless wild onions. The Blackfoot beat the bulbs into a pulp and applied it as a wet dressing to sprains and bruises.

Although the seeds are the most poisonous part of the plant, the herbage is the most common cause of livestock poisoning. *Z. elegans* may cause poisoning to livestock. The shorter species, *Z. nuttallii,* is particularly poisonous to sheep and somewhat poisonous to cattle.

The two midwestern species, *Z. elegans* and *Z. nuttallii,* seem to be less toxic than some of the other related species. Another species, *Z. gramineus,* is more common to the south.

photograph by Sylvan T. Runkel

Other common names: mullein-leaved verbena, woolly verbena

Verbena: a Latin name for any sacred herb

Stricta: meaning "strict"

Vervain family: Verbenaceae

Found throughout most of the United States in prairies, on roadsides, and in other open habitats. Flowers from late June to September.

Hoary vervain grows to a height of 3 feet. This perennial has opposite, coarsely toothed leaves and square stems. Stems branch and form a cluster of elongate branches at the top. The oval, prominently veined leaves are sessile or nearly so; they achieve a length of 4 inches. The plant is normally densely hairy.

Varying from purplish blue to rose, the flowers occur in terminal spikes that may grow up to 8 inches long. (Blooming begins at the bottom of the spike and proceeds upward, providing a long blooming period.) The flowers are nearly ½ inch long and are slightly irregular, with two upper and three lower lobes. The calyx is five-toothed, with one tooth shorter than the others.

Reproduction is mainly by seed. The seed is small and gray in color; the upper part is netted.

Some native Americans gathered the seeds, which they roasted and then ground into a flour or meal. The Omaha prepared a tea from the leaves. The Teton Dakota used this beverage as a remedy for stomach aches. In California, American Indians gathered, roasted, and ground the seeds of the blue vervain for use as meal.

The vervains are ranked as weeds by many people because they are coarse, generally unpalatable plants that thrive in dry, open habitats. Their extensive underground root systems protect these plants from severe conditions and help them act as soil anchors in eroded situations.

Vervains are among the most persistent members of the prairie flora and are common on degraded prairies. They increase in abundance when habitats are disturbed.

Other native vervains that may be found in prairies are the white vervain (*V. urticifolia*), which has small white flowers and grows in moist habitats, and the blue vervain (*V. hastata*), which has bright purple flowers and occurs in a variety of habitats. Many flower enthusiasts grow one of various garden vervains as a colorful and sometimes fragrant addition to their flower gardens.

The tops of the vervains persist throughout the winter, providing a seed source for birds, but are otherwise of only limited use as a wildlife food.

photograph by John Schwegman

Other common names: catgut, devil's shoestrings, hoary pea, North American turkey pea, Virginia tephrosia, wild sweetpea

Tephrosia: from Greek *tephros,* meaning "ash-colored or hoary"

Virginiana: meaning "of Virginia"

Legume family: Fabaceae (Leguminosae)

Found on dry, sandy soils throughout the tallgrass prairie and beyond to the east and south. Blooms June through July.

The leafy stem of goat's rue grows erect and unbranched to 2 feet tall. In most cases it is covered with soft white hairs, giving it a distinctive silvery appearance.

Compound leaves on short petioles have mostly 8 to 15 pairs of leaflets along the central leaf stem and one leaflet at the tip. The pairs of leaves toward each end tend to be smaller than those toward the center. Individual leaflets have smooth margins and are more or less oblong in shape and somewhat narrowed toward the base. They are up to 1 inch long and perhaps one-fourth as wide. These leaflets are covered with tiny, silky hairs.

This perennial has a deep taproot that branches into a series of tough, stringy, fibrous rootlets from which the name devil's shoestrings is derived.

The flowers resemble bicolored sweetpeas about ¾ inch long. The side petals, called wings, tend to be pink with purple markings. The upper petal (standard) is pale yellow. There is considerable variation in shading within the species. The flowers are borne in a dense pyramid-like terminal cluster that is 2 to 3 inches long. Each flower is on its own short stalk.

The fruit is a narrow, whitish, hairy pod about 2 inches long. This legume-type pod is lightly curved and contains several seeds.

American Indians and early settlers used the roots of goat's rue as a purgative. Indians used them as a deworming treatment.

The Cherokee drank a decoction of the root for weariness. Cherokee women washed their hair in it, believing the toughness of the roots would transfer to their hair and prevent it from falling out. For the same reason, some early ball players rubbed their hands, arms, and legs with it to toughen them.

Creek women suffering from irregular periods bathed in liquid with *T. virginiana* added to it. The Creeks also drank a cold infusion for bladder trouble and a decoction for coughing.

Early doctors used goat's rue as a cathartic, a root tonic, and an aperient. It was once considered helpful in treating syphilis and worms, and it was used as a tonic, a stimulant, and a laxative.

Some American Indians recognized the effect of the rotenone in its roots and used the plant as a poison to stun fish.

At times in the ancient past, this plant was fed to goats in an effort to increase their milk production.

This species is a nutritious constituent of prairie pastures and is relished by livestock. The plant is a sensitive indicator of good prairie quality.

photograph by John Schwegman

Other common names: drooping coneflower, gray coneflower, prairie coneflower (also applied to *R. columnifera*), weary Susan, grayhead coneflower

Ratibida: The origin of this name is not clear.

Pinnata: from Latin, meaning "featherlike"

Daisy family: Asteraceae (Compositae)

Found throughout the tallgrass prairie and dry areas elsewhere. Also commonly found along roadsides and old railroad rights-of-way. Typical coneflower-type blossoms appear from June to September.

Yellow coneflower is a tall, erect, summer perennial. Its slender, grooved stem is sometimes branched, and it is covered with fine hairs that point upward. The root system is a stout, woody rhizome.

Alternate lower leaves on long petioles are divided into three to seven leaflets. Leaflets are slender and lance-shaped and usually have coarse teeth. They may or may not have petioles. Leaves tend to droop slightly. Lower leaves may be as long as 10 inches; the upper ones are smaller.

One or several flowers may top a single stem. Each flower has its own long stalk. From five to 10 light yellow rays (petals) droop downward until they are almost parallel to the stalk. The rays are as long as 2 inches and are less than ½ inch wide. They are arranged around a cone.

The cone is actually a "disk" of flowers. Prior to the opening of the disk florets, the disk is an ashy gray, but after the florets open, the disk turns brown. The cone may be ¾ inch long and is longer than it is wide. When the center cone is crushed, it has a distinct anise scent.

The seeds are small, flattened ovals with winged margins. There is no pappus. There is sometimes a crown of hairlike material on the achene, or seed.

American Indians made a tea from the flower cones and the leaves of yellow coneflower. The Meskwaki used the root to cure toothaches.

When the plant is young, it provides good grazing for livestock.

Yellow coneflower grows readily from seed, which is usually produced abundantly. For those who would like to start a garden of prairie flowers, yellow coneflower is a good dependable starter.

This plant is often found growing in areas of former prairie where all or nearly all of the original plants have disappeared. It is a showy survivor.

photograph by Dorothy Baringer

Other common names: Indian fig

Opuntia: an old Latin name used by Pliny, probably derived from Opus, a town in ancient Greece

Compressa: from the flattened stem segments

Cactus family: Cactaceae

Found on sandy prairies and rocky terrain from the lower Great Plains across the Midwest, nearly to the East Coast. Flowering time is June and July.

This prostrate, spreading, perennial herb occurs in carpets up to 3 feet in diameter. It is normally restricted to small patches but may become a problem in overgrazed pastures in the western United States.

The root system is fibrous and branched.

The tiny, scalelike leaves quickly dry and fall. The large paddle-shaped segments that remain are flattened portions of the stem. In the axils of the small, spirally arranged leaves are clusters of bristles called glochids and often longer spines as well. The glochids easily penetrate the skin, and they are difficult to remove. Great caution should be used when handling this species.

The flower is bright yellow and large, up to 4 inches across, with numerous bright stamens. The center of the flower is often red. The flower has from 8 to 12 overlapping petals that open in sunshine and remain open for about 2 days.

The fruit is greenish or purple and contains numerous small, flattened seeds. Reproduction is by seed or by fragmentation of the stems, which root freely at nodes.

Prickly pear fruits may be peeled and the pulp eaten raw or cooked. Syrup may be made by boiling the fruit and straining the juice. In the Southwest, seeds are heated, pulverized, and used to thicken soups.

In many countries this genus is extensively cultivated for the fruits. From American Indians the Spanish explorers learned of the uses of this genus and took specimens back to Spain and to the Spanish colonies.

While they are spineless or have very soft spines, young plants are readily eaten by livestock. Older plants can be used as an emergency food for livestock if the spines are burned off or if the segments are peeled.

A second species, *O. fragilis,* the fragile prickly pear, is found less frequently in the Midwest. Unlike *O. compressa,* it has nearly cylindrical segments and more spines arising from the same point. It is more restricted in habitat and is confined largely to the Upper Midwest.

photograph by John Schwegman

Other common names: yellow Indian paintbrush

Castilleja: in honor of an early Spanish botanist, Domingo Castillejo

Sessiliflora: from Latin, meaning generally "flower without a stalk"

Snapdragon family: Scrophulariaceae

Found in dry prairies and plains from Wisconsin and Illinois to Oklahoma, Kansas, and Texas. Blooms May through July.

This soft, leafy perennial grows 6 to 12 inches tall. The stems, which usually grow in clusters, are covered with fine hairs and a whitish bloom, as if they had been powdered with ashes.

The alternate leaves have no petioles and are variable. They are usually 1 to 2 inches long. The lower leaves tend to be narrow, almost grasslike. Farther up the stem they are broader, with three narrow diverging lobes. The center lobe may also be cleft or lobed.

Large but inconspicuous flowers form dense spikes. Each flower, perhaps 1½ inches long, is a yellowish white tube with an upper lip about twice as long as the lower lip. The tip of the lower lip is often bent sharply downward.

Large floral bracts, smaller than the leaves but otherwise much like them, are light green to yellow and are shorter than the flowers.

The fruit is an oval, two-celled capsule that is perhaps ½ inch long. Each segment contains many small, net-veined seeds.

A related species, *C. coccinea,* Indian paintbrush, is fairly widespread in the tallgrass prairie biome, especially on sandy substrates. It has intense orange or crimson bracts that nearly hide the greenish yellow flowers.

The flowers of most species are considered edible; they are eaten raw. The Navajo steeped the plant in hot water and used it as a rinse for stings and insect bites. Hopi women prepared a tea of the entire plant of Indian paintbrush and drank it as a sort of contraceptive.

Members of this genus are often partial parasites, especially on the roots of asters or members of the Asteraceae family.

photograph by Linda Gucciardo

Other common names: black Samson, red sunflower

Echinacea: from the Greek, meaning "sea urchin" or "hedgehog," referring to the sharp, spiny chaff on the domelike center of this flower

Purpurea: from the Greek, meaning "purple," referring to the color of the ray flowers of some species

Daisy family: Asteraceae (Compositae)

Found in prairies and dry, open woods. Blooms late May to October.

Other species commonly found in the area are *E. angustifolia* and *E. pallida. E. pallida* blooms May to July.

Purple coneflower grows from 2 to nearly 4 feet tall, but other species may be from 2 to 3 feet tall. The ovate to lanceolate lower leaves have toothed edges and are very rough to the touch. The upper leaves and leaves of other species are without toothed edges. Leaves are 3 to 8 inches long and 1 to 3 inches wide.

The plant grows from a thick, grayish brown to black perennial root. The furrowed or ridged rootstock is ¼ to ½ inch in diameter.

The flower head has 12 to 20 spreading or drooping, purple, petal-like rays. Rays occasionally vary from purple to crimson and rarely are pale. Each ray is 1½ to 3 inches long. The center cone is more dome-shaped than cone-shaped, and it is rough and prickly to the touch. The entire flower may be 3 to 3½ inches

across. The rays of a more southern species, *E. paradoxa,* are bright yellow.

Plains Indians favored the root of purple coneflower for snakebites, bee stings, headaches, stomach cramps, toothaches, enlarged glands such as mumps, sore throats, and hydrophobia and for distemper in horses. The Sioux used freshly scraped root (as a poultice) for snakebite and for the bite of a mad dog, and they chewed pieces of rootstalk for toothache.

American Indians discovered that the plant was somewhat like a burn preventative and enabled the body to endure extreme heat. Medicine men bathed their hands and arms in the juice, then picked out meat from boiling stew. Sometimes it was used prior to sweat baths and ritual feats such as immersing hands in scalding water or holding live coals in the mouth.

A smoke treatment was used for headache in humans and for distemper in horses.

Early doctors thought purple coneflower made the body more resistent to infection, and they often used it to induce profuse sweating. They believed it had a bright future as a medicinal drug source. Modern medicine still uses extracts from this plant for treating wounds and sore throats.

The root of *E. angustifolia* has been used by the Plains Indians as a pain killer for toothaches and sore throats, since chewing the root causes the throat, tongue, and jaw to be numbed. It has also been used as a blood purifier and to treat snakebite, blood poisoning, and cancer. Burns were bathed in *E. pallida* juice to give relief from pain.

photograph by Sylvan T. Runkel

Other common names: false sunflower

Heliopsis: from Greek *helios* for "sun" and *opsis* for "appearance"

Helianthoides: from Greek, meaning "like *Helianthus,*" the sunflower

Daisy family: Asteraceae (Compositae)

Found in most of the tallgrass prairie and other open spaces, especially on dry soils. It may also be found in disturbed areas, dry woods, and dry to wet ground. It has a tendency to form clumps. Blooming time is from June to October.

This tall, leafy, short-lived perennial grows erect to 5 feet or more. The smooth stem may be branched toward the top.

Large leaves shaped somewhat like arrowheads are opposite along the stem on petioles often 1 inch or more long. The leaves are thin and smooth in one variety, thicker and rough in another. Individual leaves may be as much as 6 inches long and 2 inches across. Margins have sharp, coarse teeth.

The stem may be topped with a single flower, or it may branch into a head with many flowers. Bright, light yellow flowers appear from June to October. New flowers may be seen all through the summer, whereas most of the prairie flowers bloom only for a time and then are gone.

Individual flowers have 10 or more colorful rays. Each narrow ray is generally about ¼ inch across and 1 inch long. Rays are fertile, with a tiny, forked pistil (female flower part) at the base. The ray has no male flower parts. The dome-shaped center disk, which is yellow like the rays, may be large—nearly 1 inch across and ½ inch high. The disk flowers are fertile, bearing both stamens and pistils. The flowers generally have long stems.

Unlike those of sunflowers and coneflowers, the ray flowers of ox-eye produce fruit that yields fertile seed. The fruit is a smooth, four-sided achene (dry seed), usually without a pappus (a crown of bristles or hairs that aids in wind dissemination). Many of the Compositae have this pappus.

A closely related species, *H. scabra,* was made into a tea for treating a wide range of lung troubles. (Some consider *H. scabra* a variety of *H. helianthoides.*)

Both *H. scabra* and *H. helianthoides* have been used as ornamentals.

A variety of ox-eye is considered one of the best hardy plants for a wildflower garden border. It is considered especially suitable and valuable for planting in dry locations. A thick, bushy plant 2 to 3 feet high and 3 to 4 feet wide, it produces many deep yellow flowers.

photograph by William P. Pusateri

Other common names: beggar's lice, sticktights, tick clover

Desmodium: from Greek, meaning "long branch or chain," probably from the shape and attachment of the seedpods

Illinoense: meaning "of Illinois"

Legume family: Fabaceae (Leguminosae)

Found on Midwest prairies, often in the moist or mesic portions. Flowering time is June through September.

Tick trefoil plants are usually less than 3 feet in height but may be considerably taller when conditions are favorable. The stems tend to be spindly, sometimes erect and sometimes trailing. They are generally hairy (pubescent) and may be profusely branched or unbranched.

The perennial root system is extensive and deep. Bacteria that live in the nodules on the root take nitrogen from the air and convert it to a form plants can use. This is one way the prairie sod is enriched.

Leaves are alternately arranged along the stem and are pinnately three-parted. The smooth-margined leaflets are longish ovals; they are nearly glabrous (without hair) above and have hooked hairs below. The upper surface of the leaflet may feel somewhat sticky. The stipules at the base of the petiole are somewhat clasping.

The inflorescence is a sparsely branched raceme. The flowers have the typical legume shape but are quite small, usually less than ½ inch across. They vary in color from light pink to purplish, darkening as the plant matures. Bracts are prominently ribbed and have ciliate margins. Seedpods, flowers, and buds may appear at the same time on a single stem.

The fruits are flattened pods with a triangular segment for each seed. These pods are composed of up to seven units called articles. The joints between articles are rounded on both margins. The fruiting pods are covered with tiny, hooked hairs that cling to clothing and fur—nature's way of distributing seeds to new areas. In the fall, hikers often have trousers covered with persistent segments of the seedpods—a considerable nuisance.

Desmodium species depend on insects for pollination. Honeybees, as well as other small wild bees such as those of the genus *Halictus,* help to assure pollination.

Another fairly common member of the prairie flora is *D. canadense.* This species differs from *D. illinoense* by having a branched inflorescence with larger flowers that are rose-purple and change to blue with age. This is a more robust plant and has a fruit with one straight margin and one curved or obtusely angled margin. Articles are densely pubescent.

No uses of tick trefoil by pioneers or native Americans are known. There has been some experimentation with various species as possible forage crops, but the tightly clinging pods in late summer may limit the plants' usefulness.

Plants of this genus are largely woodland plants and grow in a wide variety of habitats. There are about 160 species of *Desmodium* worldwide, with most being found in North America.

photograph by Richard F. Trump

Other common names: Illinois acacia, prairie mimosa, pickle-weed

Desmanthus: from the Greek words *desme,* meaning "a bundle," and *anthos,* meaning "flower"

Illinoensis: meaning "of Illinois"

Legume family: Fabaceae (Leguminosae)

Found throughout the tallgrass prairie and Great Plains on both moist and dry soils, although it is more abundant in the moist depressional soils. Flowers appear from June through August but are most plentiful in July.

This erect perennial has a distinctly grooved stem that can grow to a height of 6 feet but is more commonly 2 to 4 feet tall. The alternate leaves are bipinnate and divide into 6 to 15 pinnae along each leafstalk. Each of the pinnae has 20 to 30 pairs of leaflets along its own central stalk. Despite the many parts, the total leaf is perhaps 4 inches long. The leaves are light- and touch-sensitive; they fold in strong sunlight and when touched.

From the axils of the upper leaves grow long, slender flower-stalks. Each stalk bears a ball-shaped cluster of tiny, greenish white flowers. The cluster of flowers is about ½ inch across. Each flower has five petals, each less than ⅛ inch long. The fine, long stamens projecting from each flower give the cluster a fuzzy appearance.

The fruit is a twisted or curved pod that is flat and leathery. It grows to 1½ inches long and ¼ inch across. Each pod contains two to six smooth seeds that are about ⅛ inch across, moon-shaped, and flat. Each dense seed head is usually a cluster of 20 to 30 of these pods.

Illinois bundleflower was considered a cure for any itch.

This species is often considered our most important native legume for grazing because it is high in protein. How it might be produced as a farm crop has been investigated.

It has been cultivated in gardens more for the effect of its unique seed head and foliage than for its flowers. The foliage resembles that of the mimosa, which is also a legume, but Illinois bundleflower does not have thorns.

About 40 species belong to this genus; they are found mostly in the tropics and warmer parts of the world. A dozen or so species occur in the United States.

A southwestern species, *D. leptolobus,* differs from *D. illinoensis* in that it has narrow and straight pods. It is also found in southern Missouri.

photograph by John Schwegman

Other common names: spotted St. John's-wort

Hypericum: the ancient Greek name for this genus

Punctatum: from Latin, meaning generally "dotted," for the conspicuous marking of black and clear glandular dots on its leaves and flowers

St. John's-wort family: Hypericaceae. (The family name is derived from an ancient legend that the bloodlike spots on the leaves appeared immediately after St. John was beheaded.)

Found throughout the tallgrass prairie and elsewhere on damp soils of prairies and woodland openings. Some species seem to prefer areas that are also rocky. Blooms late June to September.

This perennial grows from 1 to 5 feet tall but is usually less than 3 feet high. The sturdy stem is usually somewhat branched toward the top.

Pairs of opposite leaves without petioles often clasp the stem. The leaves are ½ to 2½ inches long and are shaped like ovals that are somewhat rounded at the tips. They are thick and have a leathery texture. The midrib is especially prominent on the underside.

Tips of the branches divide, and often further subdivide, into flowerstalks that each bear a single blossom. The result is a dense flower head of numerous blossoms.

The flowers have five pale yellow petals that are streaked with dark lines and dots. Individual flowers are generally ⅓ to ½ inch across. When fully open, the flower forms a flattish cup that has numerous yellow stamens standing out from its center. Five unequal sepals surround the base of each flower.

Since the flowers secrete no nectar, they appeal only to pollen gatherers, and they are cross-pollinated by these insects only. Tiny, blackish, cylindrical seeds are borne in a small capsule.

St. John's-wort was considered one of the most magical of all herbs for warding off evil spirits and sickness. It was the most "effective" if "smoked" in a fire kindled on the eve of St. John's Day (June 24). It was hung in windows of cottages to avert the "evil eye" and to break spells of the spirits of the dark.

According to European folklore this plant was used as a talisman against thunder and witches, but it was also useful as a treatment for weak eyes. Its calming properties were utilized for treating insomnia, bed-wetting, sleepwalking, hysteria, and other nervous conditions. It was most valued, however, as an astringent. A volatile oil extracted from the red juice was used to heal cuts and bruises. During the last century, this oil was applied to wounds in which the nerves were exposed.

When white-skinned animals browse on St. John's-wort while it is in the flowering stage, their skin becomes sensitive to sunlight, resulting in blisters and a loss of hair.

The plant tops produce a good, dark yellow dye.

The Menomini treated tuberculosis with related species, which also were mixed with raspberry root for treating kidney troubles.

photograph by LeRoy G. Pratt

Other common names: cord grass, freshwater cord grass, marsh grass, slough grass, tall marsh grass, rip gut

Spartina: from Greek *spartine,* a cord such as that made from the bark of *Spartinum.* This was probably from the strong, tough leaves.

Pectinata: from Latin, meaning "comblike," from the toothed edge of the leaf blades

Grass family: Poaceae (Gramineae)

Found on deep, heavy soil of lowlands. It may grow where water stands in the spring. This species often forms dense sods in prairie swales. Flowering time is from July into September.

This tall, warm season perennial forms a dense sod in wet areas of the prairie, often crowding out all other species. Firm, airy stems that are about ¼ inch thick at the base grow 4 to 10 feet tall. It begins growth in April and is 2 to 3 feet high by June, standing well above big bluestem and switchgrass at that time. In favorable sites, it may reach 10 feet when mature.

The root system includes heavy, woody, multibranched, creeping rhizomes. The coarse rhizomes often form a dense mat close to the surface of wet soils but also may penetrate the soil as deep as 10 feet. They are usually brownish to purplish in color.

The light green leaf blades, ranging from 12 to 30 inches long and ¼ to ⅝ inch wide, taper gradually to a whiplike point. They are flat when freshly cut but roll up when dry. A distinctive feature of the blade is its margin, which is so sharply toothed that it is as if it had spines. The margins are so sharp that the blades must be handled carefully to avoid being cut.

The flowers, as in all grasses, are very inconspicuous because they lack showy petals. They exist as flattened spikelets in two rows along the rachis.

Prairie cord grass was often used by American Indians and pioneers because its blades were so coarse and tough. The Indians thatched the roofs of their dwellings with cord grass before they added the final layer of sod. Pioneers probably used it the same way, as well as to cover corncribs and haystacks. Cord grass also provided a heavy sod for sod house construction.

One report indicates that when early settlers of Minnesota were short of fuel, they burned this grass. They twisted handfuls of grass, doubled them over to fireplace length, and tied them. An hour of preparation was needed to prepare fuel for a day.

Because of its coarse stems and rough-edged leaves, it is not readily eaten by livestock except in the spring. In hay, the stems and leaves intertwine, making it hard to handle from the stack.

Prairie cord grass provides protection for wildlife, and muskrats eat its roots. Related species along Gulf Coast marshes furnish food for geese.

The mats of coarse, woody, thick, branching rhizomes that form in the upper inches of soil beneath stands of prairie cord grass are good for soil conservation. It is sometimes cultivated around the edges of ponds and artificial lakes. Most propagation is by rhizomes because viable seeds are seldom produced.

photograph by Ted Van Bruggen

Other common names: scurf pea

Psoralea: from Greek, meaning "scurfy" or "scabby," because of the glandular spots on the leaves, stems, and calyx

Argophylla: meaning "silvery-leaved"

Legume family: Fabaceae (Leguminosae)

Found in drier parts of prairies in the western portion of the tallgrass biome. Flowers late June through early August.

This attractive member of the tallgrass prairie flora is erect, widely branched, and densely hairy. The white appressed hairs give it a distinctive silvery color. The entire plant is generally less than 2 feet high, but it may exceed 3 feet.

The stem, which often zigzags, supports alternate palmately compound leaves of three to five short-stalked leaflets. The leaflets are pointed ovals with smooth margins.

The deep purple flower petals scarcely exceed the longest calyx lobe. These typical pea-like flowers, usually only about ⅛ inch across, are arranged in spikes and are supported by a peduncle (flower or fruit stem) that is longer than the leaves.

The ovate seedpod, containing one to two seeds, is covered with silky hairs. The plant spreads by creeping rhizomes (underground stems that root at the nodes). They are somewhat thickened and have a mealy texture.

The Meskwaki used this species as a tea for chronic constipation. The Cheyenne made a fever-reducing tea by steeping finely ground leaves and stems in boiling water.

While *P. esculenta* has long been used as an important food source by American Indians of the prairie country, the edibility of some of the *Psoralea* species is suspect. Many reports have been made of cattle and horses being poisoned by grazing on *P. tenuiflora,* the slender-flowered scurf pea.

P. argophylla is suspected of severely poisoning a child who ate a quantity of its seeds. However, at present there is no experimental or research evidence to support the suspected poisoning cases.

The beautiful silvery gray color of this entire plant adds yet another dimension to the attractive color diversity of the prairie!

Of about 120 species worldwide, 30 species of this genus are in North America. They range from annual to perennial in duration.

photograph by Randall A. Maas

Other common names: five-finger, glandular cinquefoil, white cinquefoil

Potentilla: from Latin, a diminutive form of "powerful," probably applied because of the significant medical powers once attributed to another species of this genus

Arguta: from Latin, meaning "sharp," referring to the sharp teeth of the leaf margins

Rose family: Rosaceae

Found throughout the tallgrass prairies and on rocky or alluvial soils of other open areas. Blooms June and July.

This rather coarse perennial produces erect, unbranched stems that grow to heights of 3 feet. The stems have a dense covering of clammy, brown hairs. The root system is a stout, scaly rhizome.

Basal leaves carried on slender petioles are cut into 7 to 11 oval segments. The end 3 leaflets are slightly larger than the rest. The leaflets are downy beneath and are strongly veined. The coarse teeth of the leaf margins may also be toothed. Leaves along the stems have fewer segments and have either no petioles or very short ones.

The branching flower head is a loose cluster containing many whitish or creamy flowers that appear in June and July. The flowers of most *Potentilla* species are yellow. Individual flowers, less than ¾ inch across, have five broad oval petals. The stamens (male flower parts) are carried in five groups on the thickened margin of the flower's center disk.

The tiny seeds are smooth and somewhat fiddle-shaped.

The Ojibwa powdered the root of this species, put the dry or moistened powder on duck down, and applied the down to a wound to control bleeding.

Numerous other cinquefoils have been used in medicine. Shrubby cinquefoil (*P. fruiticosa*) leaves have been used to prepare a substitute for tea. The Ojibwa treated stomach cramps with marsh cinquefoil (*P. palustris*).

Silverweed (*P. anserina*) roots, which taste like parsnips or sweet potatoes, were eaten by native Americans, settlers, and Europeans. It was considered a good treatment for difficult menstruation, for diarrhea, and for piles. A teaspoon of dried herb to 1 cup boiling water, with honey added, was an excellent gargle for a sore throat. A strong distillation was said to take away freckles, pimples, and sunburn.

Because of a tendency for roots to develop at nodes and form new plants, silverweed can survive overgrazing. It is used to protect overgrazed streambanks and water holes.

Shrubby cinquefoil has a wide range of habitats. It is found growing in open areas all the way from the Midwest in the United States to the Arctic in northern Canada and Alaska.

photograph by Randall A. Maas

Other common names: thimbleweed, red tassel flower

White prairie clover: *Petalostemum candidum* (Willd.) Michx.

Other common names: thimbleweed, white tassel flower

Petalostemum: from the Greek, meaning "petal and stamen," referring to the way the petals and stamens are joined

Purpureum: meaning "purple"

Candidum: meaning "shining white"

Legume family: Fabaceae (Leguminosae)

Both of these *Petalostemum* species are found throughout the Midwest in native prairies and prairie relicts on well-drained or dry soils. The two species are frequently found together. They bloom from June to September.

These perennial plants often occur in patches. As many as 8 to 10 stems may arise from the deep and spreading perennial root. Slender, erect stems grow from 1 to 2 feet tall. The short-petioled leaves have an odd number of ¼- to ¾-inch leaflets: three to five for *P. purpureum,* five to nine for *P. candidum.*

The flowers are not typical legume flowers, since they have one large petal and four smaller ones, all on slender claws. The individual flowers, about ¼ inch long, cluster tightly around a cylinder-like cone. The small flowers start as a circle or ring around the base of the head and work upward as the season advances. The flower spike is from ½ to 2 inches long.

Although called purple prairie clover, *P. purpureum* usually is not purple but is more roseate, pink, or red. White prairie clover, *P. candidum,* has white flowers.

American Indians used the prairie clover plant medicinally by applying a tea made of the leaves to open wounds. The bruised leaves, steeped in water, were also applied to wounds. When mixed with hot water, the pulverized root made a healthful drink that was used as a preventative medicine. The Pawnee used the plants as a prophylactic. Settlers mixed the bark of white oak and the flowers of prairie clover to make a drink they used as a medicine for diarrhea.

In Ireland and Scotland, prairie clover seeds were ground into a flour from which a nutritious bread was made. Comanches chewed the roots and made a tea from the leaves. The Oglala used these plants to prepare a tea, and the Ponca chewed the roots for their pleasant taste.

The prairie clovers enrich the soil by adding nitrogen to it. They are high on the list of palatable and valuable forage plants.

Indian women gathered the tough, elastic stems to make brooms, and the Pawnee name for these plants translates as "broom weed."

photograph by Randall A. Maas

Other common names: rose milkweed, silkweed, water nerve root, white Indian hemp

Asclepias: from the name of the Greek god of healing and medicine

Incarnata: from Latin, for "flesh," referring to the flesh-colored flowers

Milkweed family: Asclepiadaceae

Found throughout the tallgrass prairie region in moist soil at the edges of prairie potholes or marshes. Blooms July through August.

Swamp milkweed is a tall perennial; it grows to a height of over 5 feet. The glabrous stem is solitary or clustered. A small amount of milky juice exudes from a broken stem.

The deep green leaves are 3 to 6 inches long. They are lanceolate or obovate and have petioles ¼ to ½ inch long.

The root system has numerous threadlike roots, 6 to 8 inches long, extending from a sturdy crown that has many buds.

The flowers are pale pink to rose-purple, rarely whitish, and have short hoods. The hoods equal the length of the anthers.

The erect pods are 2 to 4 inches long and contain many plumed seeds.

Milkweeds have a long medicinal history. Canadian Indians drank an infusion of the ground root to provide temporary sterility. The Meskwaki made a tea of the root and used it "to expel worms in an hour." Some tribes burned off the plumes, then ground the seeds and steeped them in water for use in drawing the poison out of a rattlesnake bite.

Milkweeds also served as food, and some tribes cultivated them. The Ojibwa used the flowers and buds in soups. The Chippewa cut and stewed the flowers and ate them like preserves. Some American Indians cooked young pods with buffalo meat. The common milkweed (*A. syriaca*) was the source of a sugar. The Sioux collected the flowers in the morning while they were still dew-covered. These flowers were squeezed to get a juice that was boiled until it yielded a palatable brown sugar.

During World War II, the milky sap was tested as a rubber substitute, and the plumes of the seed heads were tried as a replacement for kapok in life preservers. In Europe, the silky fibers of the plumes have been used for making hats and for stuffing pillows.

Milkweeds are characteristic of the prairie ecosystem. Some are exceedingly rare—the presence of these and other prairie plants gives ecologists the information needed to determine the quality of the prairie.

photograph by Randall A. Maas

Other common names: rosinweed, turpentine plant, polar plant

Silphium: an old Greek generic name relating to the resinous juice

Laciniatum: Latin for "slashed"

Daisy family: Asteraceae (Compositae)

Found throughout the Midwest and to the south on mesic prairies. Blooms July through August.

Growing from a thick, deeply penetrating taproot, the compass plant may reach a height of 8 feet. The leaves grow to 1 foot long and 6 inches wide. The irregularly lobed basal leaves tend to orient themselves in a general north-south direction, hence, the common name. The leaves on the stem are clasping and have fewer lobes.

Yellow flower heads 3 to 4 inches across alternate up the stem. They resemble those of a wild sunflower and contribute to the late season show of color on the prairie. Ray flowers, numbering 20 to 30 per head, are up to 2 inches long.

The plant is propagated by numerous seeds that mature by early fall.

This genus is generally listed in ancient medicine as a tonic, a diaphoretic, and an alterative. The smaller roots of *S. laciniatum* were cooked and the liquid was drunk as an emetic. Early settlers used it internally to treat chronic rheumatism, scrofula, and glandular enlargements. The dried leaves were used as an antispas-modic, diuretic, expectorant, and emetic. It was valued for curing dry, obstinate coughs and for treating intermittent fevers. The Pawnee made a decoction of the pounded root for general debility.

The Omaha and the Ponca avoided camping wherever *S. laciniatum* grew abundantly because they believed that lightning was prevalent in such a place. Sometimes they burned the dried root during electrical storms to act as a charm against a lightning strike.

It was also used as a tonic for horses. The Dakota used it to worm horses.

An unspecified species of *Silphium* was used by the Creek and by traders to cleanse teeth and sweeten breath.

When in bloom, the compass plant forms a gummy material along the upper third of the main stem. This resinous material (hence, the name rosinweed) was used by American Indians as chewing gum. Pioneer children on their way to and from country school also took advantage of this free prairie chewing gum. Chewing the gum from *S. perfoliatum,* a related species, helped to prevent vomiting.

Compass plant seems to be preferred by cattle, so most grazed prairies are devoid of this member of the flora. *S. perfoliatum* was considered as a possible fodder in the Soviet Union.

S. integrifolium, a close relative of *S. laciniatum,* has paired, rough leaves. It is found on prairies from Ohio to Minnesota and south to Louisiana and Texas.

photograph by Bob Moats

Other common names: Indian plantain, prairie Indian plantain

Cacalia: from an ancient name, the meaning of which was lost in antiquity

Tuberosa: from Latin, meaning "tuberous," referring to the thickened roots

Daisy family: Asteraceae (Compositae)

Found throughout the central part of the tallgrass prairie from Ohio and western Ontario to Minnesota and south to Alabama, Louisiana, and Texas. It occurs mostly in or near wet prairies and marshes. Blooms from June to August.

This perennial herb grows 2 to 6 feet high; stems are erect, green, and glabrous. The thick lower leaves are 4 to 8 inches long and 1 to 3 inches wide. They are ovate or pointed elliptic, with five to nine veins that all come together at the point. These lower leaves sometimes have toothed edges but are mostly entire, and they have long petioles. Upper leaves are sessile or have short petioles; they are sometimes lobed and toothed toward the apex.

The generally flat-topped inflorescence is made up of many small white flower heads. The heads are composed of five tubular disk florets, each about ⅙ inch across. The five-parted corolla is deeply cleft.

It is not known whether the large tuberous root of this plant was used by either American Indians or pioneers, but it is certain that the plant was noticed. At least one unverified account suggests that it was used for food.

Three other species of *Cacalia* may also be found in the central prairie region, but they are usually found in low, moist woodland areas. Occasionally some are found in dry to wet open woodlands and woodland borders or in the edges of wet prairies. Included here are sweet Indian plantain, *C. suaveolens;* great Indian plantain, *C. muhlenbergii;* and pale Indian plantain, *C. atriplicifolia.*

The chief identifying features of the Indian plantains are their leaf sizes and shapes. For example, *C. suaveolens* has halberd-shaped or lanceolate triangle-shaped leaves with fine toothed edges. The leaves are large, from 4 to 10 inches long and 2 to 6 inches wide. *C. muhlenbergii* has very large, thin, green, rounded or somewhat kidney-shaped leaves with angular edges. The basal leaves of this species may be from 1 to 2 feet across. *C. atriplicifolia* has whitish green, angular-lobed, fan-shaped leaves that are up to 6 inches wide. While all four species of *Cacalia* are called Indian plantain, leaves of the tuberous Indian plantain are the only leaves that resemble the typical plantain leaf shape.

photograph by Randall A. Maas

Other common names: early mesquite

Buchloe: from Greek *bous,* meaning "cow," and *cloe,* meaning "grass," a Greek rendition of buffalo grass

Dactyloides: from Greek *dactylos,* meaning "finger," and *oid,* meaning "like," perhaps for the appearance of the leaves or for a resemblance to *Dactylis,* the genus of orchardgrass. (This is the only species in the genus.)

Grass family: Poaceae (Gramineae)

Found in the Great Plains, mostly on heavy soils of dry areas. It does not tolerate dense shade or sandy soil. As a native plant, it is found only on the western edge of the tallgrass prairie. Flowering is usually early—in mid-May to June. Seeds are mature in July.

Buffalo grass is a warm season, shortgrass perennial. It is more drought and heat resistant than most grasses. Growing only 4 to 6 inches tall, the leaves often grow so close to the ground that this species survives the close grazing that decreases other species. In fact, overgrazing of tallgrass prairies increases the density of this species.

The fine leaves are less than ⅛ inch wide and 3 to 6 inches long. They are rather dense and flat and tend to curl. A covering of fine hairs gives a gray-green appearance to the leaf, which turns to a light straw color when dry.

It spreads by surface runners called stolons. The profuse branching of the stolons creates a dense sod mat.

Flowers are male or female; there is usually only one kind per plant. Male flowers are borne on stems extending 1 or 2 inches above the leaves. They occur in two-rowed clusters on one stem (somewhat resembling those of blue grama grass).

Female flowers occur in groups that are commonly called burs. Sometimes only slightly above the ground and often difficult to see, the female flowers occur on short stems that are hidden among the leaves. These flowers may be partially covered by the inflated sheaths of the upper leaves.

Flower heads usually include two burs on a common stalk. A bur seldom produces more than four seeds. By mid-to-late July, the seeds are mature, but they may lay dormant for years under the arid conditions of their native habitat. Seeds are small, with 40,000 to 50,000 seeds to the pound.

Early settlers of the Great Plains probably made their sod houses from the dense sod mats formed by buffalo grass as well as from the sod mats of prairie cord grass. The dense sod of buffalo grass makes it important in erosion control; it is also suitable for public picnic areas, airport runways, and lawns.

Livestock finds buffalo grass good grazing all year long except during the dry-period dormancy. Confronted with a shortage of hay, early pioneers on the Great Plains turned their cattle loose to forage for themselves on the apparently barren range. They were surprised to find the cattle plump and in good condition in the spring. Livestock survived nicely on the native shortgrasses, particularly buffalo grass.

photograph by Ted Van Bruggen

Other common names: bullgrass, gamagrass, sesame grass

Tripsacum: from Greek, meaning to "thresh" or "rub," probably because the fertile spike with its large seeds can be broken up so easily

Dactyloides: from Greek, meaning "finger-like"; also from an ancient name for some grasses

Grass family: Poaceae (Gramineae)

Found in southeastern Nebraska and southern Iowa, east to the Atlantic coast, and south to the Gulf. Usually found in moist sites such as banks of streams, edges of waterways, and around prairie potholes and wet meadows, where it may be associated with big bluestem. In the native prairie, it will often be found in dense stands in the areas that lie between slough grass and switchgrass. The flowering spikes may produce seed from July to September.

Eastern gamagrass, the giant of the grasses, grows from 3 to 9 feet tall. It is a native warm season perennial that spreads by thick-jointed, robust rhizomes as well as by large cornlike seeds.

It is a bunchgrass that grows in clumps up to 4 feet across. The leaf blades are up to 24 inches long and from 1 to 1½ inches wide.

Seed is produced from July to September in seed heads that are 6- to 10-inch long terminal spikes. From one to three of these spikes make up the individual seed head. The upper two-thirds or three-fourths of each spike is the pollen-bearing male part: the lower one-fourth to one-third is the female part. The female part is made up of short-jointed segments (each almost as big as a grain of corn) that break apart as the seeds mature. Each segment contains one seed.

Because of its large size, broad, long leaves, and large individual grains, some authorities have believed that this grass could have been one of the ancestors of corn (*Zea mays*). At present, however, this theory is largely discounted, even though, experimentally, eastern gamagrass has been artificially crossed with corn.

Eastern gamagrass is widespread, but it is not common enough to be considered an important forage grass. However, this grass produces a nutritious, palatable, and productive forage, which makes it of interest to researchers. It has been termed by some as our most productive hay grass. Because of its productivity and its close relationship to corn, eastern gamagrass will likely merit continued interest and study.

Because of its unusual appearance and size, this grass is sometimes planted in flower gardens and is used in landscaping.

photograph by William P. Pusateri

Other common names: terrell grass, Virginia lyme grass

Elymus: from a Greek name for a kind of grain, meaning generally "to roll up," referring to the lemma and palea, which are tightly rolled about the seed

Virginicus: meaning "of Virginia"

Grass family: Poaceae (Gramineae)

Found on moist prairies as well as woodlands. It grows in denser shade and prefers heavier and more fertile soil than Canada wild rye (*E. canadensis*), which is found throughout the continent. Virginia wild rye is most often found in lowland areas. As implied by the species name, it is found in the eastern portion of the tallgrass prairie and east to the seacoast. Blooms from late June into October.

This perennial bunchgrass grows to a height of 3 feet. Rough to the touch, the leaves vary from 5 to 14 inches long and are up to ⅔ inch wide.

Flower spikes are robust and upright and have straight awns. Each spikelet contains two to three flowers. Empty scales (glumes) are lance-shaped and up to 1 inch long.

This highly variable species is often divided into several varieties. Some varieties have short awns and smooth spikes, others have bristly or hairy spikes and long awns.

In general, the seed heads of Virginia wild rye are stiffly straight and upright, while the seed heads of Canada wild rye are curved and drooping. It may require 73,000 seeds of Virginia wild rye to make a pound.

The grains are edible, but their long awns must be singed off before they can be used. Pinole, a natural flour, is made from this and other seeds.

Virginia wild rye is palatable and makes good forage and hay. It is a cool season grass, so it furnishes fall and spring pasture. Sometimes it is seeded in warm season grass mixtures to extend grazing seasons. It can be used in pure stands in early fall for winter pastures.

A fungus called ergot may be a problem, however, if this grass is not harvested early. This fungus (*Claviceps purpurea*) infects the grass and forms a black mass that replaces the ovary of the grass flower and becomes several times longer than the fruit. It may cause abortion and other ill effects in cattle. Ergot may also occur in other grasses, such as Canada wild rye and bromegrass.

photograph by George Ceolla

Other common names: none known

Calamovilfa: from Greek *calamos,* a reed, and *vilfa,* an early name applied to a genus of grasses

Longifolia: meaning "long leaves"

Grass family: Poaceae (Gramineae)

Found wherever extensive deposits of sand are located. This handsome perennial grass is usually found at the top of a dune, where it is among the first plants to begin stabilization. Although nearly exclusive to sand, it is also found in loess deposits. Sand reed is found in Wisconsin and Illinois and west to Alberta and Colorado. Blooming time is June to September.
Calamovilfa longifolia is divided into two varieties: var. *longifolia,* which is distributed widely in the Midwest, and var. *magna,* which is restricted mainly to the shores of the Great Lakes but has also worked its way south in the Mississippi River valley to southeastern Iowa.
The only other species of *Calamovilfa* found in North America is restricted to the Eastern Seaboard.

This grass may reach an overall height of 7 feet. Sand reed's extensive rhizome system makes it well adapted to stabilizing sand dunes, and it is occasionally planted for that purpose. One identifying characteristic is the very sharp protrusion at the plant base.
Leaves are long and linear and taper to a long, thread-like point. The stem is stout and has pubescent sheaths.

The seed head, or panicle, may be over a foot in length. It characteristically has a bract at the base that is nearly as long as the panicle. Var. *longifolia* has a contracted panicle; var. *magna* has an open panicle. The callus has a heavy beard—a feature that is helpful for identifying the species.

While this grass is not considered an especially good forage, livestock will eat the tender spring growth and the dry fall forage. Other forage is preferred, however, and will be eaten first.
It is said that Chief Crazy Horse wore the panicle of sand reed on his head instead of the more traditional feather. This surely would have caused him to stand out in any group, since the panicle commonly is more than a foot long.

photograph by Ted Van Bruggen

Other common names: prairie white-fringed orchid, western greenish-fringed orchis

Platanthera: from Greek, meaning "broad anthers." (This plant is sometimes placed in a separate fringed orchid genus called *Blephariglottis,* Latin for "eyelid tongued," in obvious reference to the fringed lip of the flower.)

Leucophaea: from Latin *leuco,* meaning "white," and *phaea,* meaning "dusky." This is in reference to the appearance of having been dusted with a whitish powder resembling ashes.

Orchid family: Orchidaceae

Found in wet prairies of the Middle West and in swamps, especially tamarack bogs, to the east. Blooms June through July.

This once common member of the orchid family grows 1 to 3 feet tall on a stout, unbranched stem. The stem is angled in cross section. The perennial rootstock is fibrous and fleshy and is somewhat tuberous.

Smooth, alternate leaves are narrow elongated ovals with blunt tips. Leaves are usually 4 to 8 inches long and often 1 inch wide. Upper leaves are considerably smaller than lower ones.

A thick but loosely arranged cylindrical flower spike up to 5 inches long and 2 to 3 inches wide consists of creamy white to greenish white flowers. Each flower is about 1 inch long.

Individual flowers are typical of the orchid family; they have three colored sepals and three petals. The sepals, all alike, form the upper part of the flower. The two lateral petals are alike; each is about ¼ inch long. The lower petal forms a lip about ½ inch long. The lip is deeply cut into three wedge-shaped lobes. The center lobe is about as broad as it is long. The two side lobes are noticeably narrower. A delicate, threadlike fringe on the lobes of the lip gives the flower a somewhat ragged appearance. The base of the lip forms a spur that may be 1½ inches long. Small leaflike bracts are at the base of each flower.

Pollination is by moths and butterflies. When these insects seek the nectar, pear-shaped masses of pollen become stuck on their heads, thus ensuring the transfer of pollen to other plants.

The fruit is a three-angled capsule with a single cell that contains many tiny, spindle-shaped seeds.

A plant of this genus, *P. bracteata,* was used by the Ojibwa as a sort of love charm. They would secretly put some of it into food as an aphrodisiac (the person who was to eat it was not told because such use was considered unfair). *P. dilatata* was used by Potawatomi women as a love charm; it was rubbed or painted on the cheek to help secure a good husband. It was also thought to help men obtain a good wife.

Prairie fringed orchis continues to decline in abundance. Its faint, lovely scent was mentioned by people who visited the unbroken prairie. Finding it today is a treasured experience.

The smaller purple-fringed orchis, *P. psycodes,* usually is found in wetter habitats than where *P. leucophaea* is found. A very similar species, *P. praeclara,* the western fringed orchid, occurs in the western portion of the tallgrass prairie.

photograph by Tomma Lou Maas

Other common names: curly cup, rosinweed, sticky heads, tar weed

Grindelia: in honor of David Hieronymus Grindel, a Russian botanist at the beginning of the 19th century

Squarrosa: from the botanical term *squarrose,* meaning "having stiff spreading bracts," in reference to the many bracts surrounding the base of each flower

Daisy family: Asteraceae (Compositae)

Found in dry prairies and in moist, degraded or disturbed areas. Blooms from July to September.

The short, stout, multibranched stem of this short-lived perennial seldom reaches 3 feet tall. In some cases, the stem may have a reddish cast to its otherwise dark green color. The deep taproot makes gumweed extremely drought resistant.

The leaves, although variable, are generally oblong with pointed tips. Mostly 1½ inches long and ½ inch wide, they are a glistening dark green. Translucent spots of sticky or gummy sap are apparent. Leaves alternate along the stem and have toothed margins. Upper leaves clasp the stem, while lower ones may have short petioles. The lower leaves often drop by flowering time.

Each upper branch usually bears a solitary bright yellow flower that is about 1 inch across. Both the center disk and the 25 to 40 straplike rays are yellow.

The numerous narrow bracts covering the base of the flower are recurved and are gummy with a gluelike resinous substance.

The fruit is a short, thick seed with four or five ribs and two to three stiff awns. The seeds are light gray. They are feathered, curved, and somewhat right-angled and have longitudinal lines.

American Indians used gumweed extract to treat asthma, bronchitis, colic, and skin rash. Early settlers used it for treating bronchial spasms, whooping cough, asthma, kidney troubles, and rashes caused by poison ivy or poison oak. The asthma treatment was powdered flower heads rolled into cigarettes.

Leaves, dried or green, were believed to make excellent tea for the treatment of indigestion, bronchial troubles, itching, colic, poison oak, and urinary ailments. American Indians used such a tea for liver troubles. A poultice of the plant was applied to arthritic joints.

A decoction of flowering tops and leaves was once used to treat gonorrhea, pneumonia, smallpox, and lung disease. The Dakota made a decoction for children with colic. The Ponca used this species for treating tuberculosis. The Pawnee boiled the tops and leaves to make a wash for saddle galls and other sores on horses' backs.

For treating poison ivy, an extract was prepared by placing freshly gathered leaves and flowers in a small amount of simmering water for about 15 minutes. In recent medicine (it may still be available), a fluid extract of two species was used as an external treatment for poison ivy rash.

When growing in areas where the soil is high in selenium, the plant may be poisonous to livestock.

photograph by Ted Van Bruggen

Other common names: nodding wild rye, rye grass, Canada lyme grass

Elymus: derived from the Greek *elymos,* the name for a kind of grain that has the lemma and palea tightly rolled about the seed

Canadensis: meaning "of Canada"

Grass family: Poaceae (Gramineae)

Found mostly on dry, sandy or rocky soils throughout the tallgrass prairie and on shaded bottomlands of the Great Plains. Seed heads may be seen in July and August.

A similar species, *E. virginicus,* with a shorter and erect seed head, is less common to the west. The two species may be found together and they sometimes hybridize.

Canada wild rye is a large, perennial bunchgrass that tends to be more coarse than many of its close relatives. It grows 2 to 5 feet tall. Growth starts early and often continues through the summer if moisture and temperature are favorable. In unfavorable years, growth may resume in the fall after a period of summer dormancy. Grass maturity may be reached in July.

Almost 1 inch across and 12 inches long, leaf blades are thick and flat. The upper blade surface is rough to the touch and tends to curl inward near the tip. Their green color appears to be somewhat powdered with a whitish bloom. Where the leaf blade joins the sheath, an earlike lobe extends from the leaf margins to clasp the stem.

Coarse-appearing seed heads may be 10 or more inches long and nearly 1 inch across. Arching seed heads occur at the top of slender, unbranched stems. Spikelets are usually in sets of three or four. They spread away from the stem at the base of the seed head. Some space often occurs between spikelets. The narrow glumes are covered with stiff, rough hairs and tipped with an awn about as long as the glume itself. The rough awns of the lemma are about 1 inch long and generally curve outward.

Compared to most grasses, seeds are relatively large and light, usually requiring slightly more than 100,000 to weigh a pound.

Persisting through the winter, seed heads are a frequent food of wildlife. Native Americans used the seeds as food, but efforts to harvest them were generally regarded as more than the low yield was worth.

Early vigorous growth and a fibrous, wide-spreading root system make Canada wild rye a valuable ground cover. It was an important part of prairie pastures.

photograph by Randall A. Maas

Other common names: button snakeroot, gayfeather

Liatris: meaning unknown; its origin lost in the mists of antiquity

Pycnostachya: from the Greek *pyhnos,* meaning "dense" or "thick"

Daisy family: Asteraceae (Compositae)

Found throughout the tallgrass prairie biome, often in thick stands on damp prairies and open bottomlands. Flowering begins in July and may continue until frost.

Several similar species are found in the tallgrass prairie. Some species favor drier sites and are common on roadsides.

This dramatic plant is one of the most conspicuous of the prairie inhabitants. Its leafy stem grows erect and unbranched to a height of 5 feet.

The narrow leaves on the lower two-thirds of the plant are so crowded that to the casual observer they may appear spiraled rather than closely alternate. Lower leaves are larger—up to 4 inches long and ½ inch wide—than those farther up the stem. Both the stem and leaves usually display short, stiff hairs.

The perennial rootstock is a rounded corm with a fibrous covering.

The top two-thirds of blazing star is a spike of rose-purple, thistle-like flowers that are given a somewhat fuzzy appearance by extended white stamens (male flower parts) and pistils (female flower parts). Flowering starts at the top of the spike and moves progressively downward. The oblong flower head has a mass of 5 to 12 tubular florets that somewhat resemble those of horsemint. A dense circle of bracts surrounds the base of each flower head. The tips of these long, pointed bracts tend to spread and curve back toward their bases. Bracts of this species may have a purplish tinge.

The slender seeds are usually less than ¼ inch long. The seed narrows toward the base and is tipped with a set of soft bristles about as long as the seed itself. Close examination of the seed shows 10 ribs or ridges.

The roots of blazing star have been described as having the flavor of carrots.

Related species were used extensively. The Pawnee boiled the leaves and corms of *L. scariosa* to prepare a decoction for children with diarrhea. The Meskwaki used this species for urinary trouble. Flower heads were mixed with shelled corn and were used to prepare horses for races. The Omaha tribe chewed the corm and blew the resulting paste into horses' nostrils to increase their endurance.

L. squarrosa was used as a diuretic, a tonic, a stimulant, and as a decoction for gonorrhea, kidney trouble, and uterine diseases.

Blazing star and related species have been used as garden ornamentals.

photograph by LeRoy G. Pratt

Other common names: sometimes called Turk's-cap lily, tiger lily, and Canada lily

Lilium: classical name for lilies, probably originating in ancient Greek or Persian usage

Michiganense: meaning "of Michigan"

Lily family: Liliaceae

Found throughout the tallgrass prairie biome in prairie swales, moist roadside ditches, and open lowland woods. Blooms July through August.

Plants grow to over 5 feet high from perennial, scaly bulbs and rootstalks. Leaves, which are normally less than 6 inches long, occur in whorls. They are rather swordlike and have smooth margins. The stem often branches at the tip to form additional flowerstalks.

The orange-red flowers are large, up to 3 inches across, with petals so conspicuously reflexed (curved backward) that their tips may touch the base of the flower. Dark spots on the inside surface of the six petals are characteristic of this species. Protruding beyond the petals are six bright red anthers (pollen sacs) and the end of the pistil. The number of blossoms per plant ranges from a few in younger plants to over 30 in old specimens.

This species is often called Turk's-cap lily, but Turk's-cap lily (*L. superbum,* or *L. canadense* ssp. *michiganense*) has a more eastern distribution and has a pronounced green streak inside each petal. In the flower, these streaks form a green star.

Another native but considerably less common lily species is the wood lily (*L. philadelphicum*), which is smaller, growing to a height of less than 3 feet, and has upright blossoms. It resembles the Michigan lily in flower color, and it also has spots on the petals and has leaves in whorls. Its petals, however, are not curved back, and the anthers protrude little if at all beyond the petals. It grows in more acid soils and in drier sites than the Michigan lily. In spite of its name, the wood lily is usually found on the prairie (see wood lily, p. 111).

The tiger lily (*L. tigrinum*) is similar but has alternate leaves and a smooth, shiny, black berrylike structure in the leaf axil. These are vegetative propagules, which drop to the ground and form new plants. The tiger lily is an introduction from Asia that sometimes escapes cultivation and grows along roads.

Seeds of these species are borne in dry capsules with three compartments. Two rows of densely packed seeds occur in each compartment. However, the fruiting body of *L. tigrinum* rarely if ever forms in the United States.

Another non-native lily commonly found along roadsides is the European day lily (*Hemerocallis fulva*).

The white, scaly bulb of the wood lily is edible. Bulbs of the Canada lily (*L. canadense*), and probably other species, were cooked or used to thicken soup by various tribes of native Americans. Some tribes used a tea made from the bulbs to treat snakebite. When chewed to a paste, the flower of the tiger lily was a treatment for spider bites.

photograph by LeRoy G. Pratt

Other common names: none known

Froelichia: named for Joseph Froelich, a German botanist

Floridana: meaning "of Florida"

Amaranth family: Amaranthaceae

Found throughout the tallgrass biome where suitable habitat can be located. The special habitat requirements make this plant uncommon in the tallgrass prairie region. It requires open, dry, sandy ground and is usually found in association with little blue-stem, sandbur, dwarf dandelion, Indian chickweed, and sheep sorrel. Blooms from July to September.

Cottonweed is a stout annual that is unbranched or has a few well-developed branches. Heights of 6 feet can be reached, but it is more commonly less than 3 feet tall. The entire plant, especially the inflorescence, has a woolly appearance. The root system is shallow, which is common in annuals.

Leaves are opposite and sessile and normally have smooth margins. They are up to 5 inches long.

Flowers are clustered into dense terminal spikes that are up to 5 inches long. Normally, several spikes are found on each plant. The five-lobed calyx, which is very woolly, often obscures the flower and seeds. The crest of the calyx is continuous and dentate (toothed).

Seeds are numerous, and they germinate well, making the plant locally abundant in sandy areas.

Cottonweed does not seem to have been used for medicinal purposes, and it has only been sparsely cultivated.

A closely related plant, *F. gracilis,* is smaller and has shorter leaves and a calyx with distinct spines. In the Upper Midwest, it is much less common than *F. floridana.*

photograph by Kitty Kohout

Other common names: none known

Helianthus: from the Greek *helios* for "sun" and *anthos* for "flower" (hence sunflower) because the flowering heads of this genus tend to turn with the sun each day

Maximiliani: named after Prinz Maximilian van Wied-Neu (1782–1867), who made extensive scientific explorations in both North and South America and discovered this plant

Daisy family: Asteraceae (Compositae)

Found throughout most of the central tallgrass prairie on a variety of sites, but it is most commonly found on rich prairies and heavier soils from Minnesota and Saskatchewan to Missouri, Oklahoma, and Texas. Blooms from July to October.

Maximilian sunflower grows erect, either singly or in a cluster of stems, from a fleshy or thickened rhizome. The gray-green stems may be 3 to 8 feet tall.

The 3- to 7-inch long, narrow, trough-shaped, lanceolate leaves are the most noticeable identifying characteristic. These gray-green leaves are rough on both sides and typically curve downward in a sickle shape. They are acute at both ends and may be sessile or have a short petiole. Leaves are mostly alternate; the lower leaves may be opposite.

The deep yellow flower heads may be few or numerous. They are 2 to 3 inches across, with 15 to 30 ray flowers and rough, stout peduncles.

Maximilian sunflower is a showy and attractive plant, and it has been cultivated in some areas. The cultivated strain is larger (up to 12 feet high) and more showy than the wild strain. Occasionally, the cultivated strain has escaped into the wild.

The common sunflower (*H. annuus*) is native to North America. Domesticated by American Indians, it is now used as a crop worldwide. It is important in Egypt, Russia, India, Turkey, Hungary, and Peru as well as in North America.

Other sunflowers commonly found in the tallgrass prairie include *H. grosseseratus,* sawtooth sunflower, with large serrations on the leaves; *H. giganteus,* with stems that grow to 10 feet high and are often purple; *H. decapetalus,* thin-leaved sunflower, with thin, smooth leaves; *H. tuberosus,* Jerusalem artichoke, with egg-shaped leaves; and *H. laetiflorus,* showy sunflower, with blunt bracts and lance-shaped leaves.

Natural hybridization commonly occurs between the various wild sunflower species, which results in interesting variations.

The seeds of the sunflowers have served as food for man, livestock, poultry, and wildlife. They are widely used for wild bird feed. A fine oil can be extracted from the seeds; it is used in cooking, for making soap, and for various industrial uses.

A fiber used for textiles has been obtained from the strong, coarse stalks, and a yellow dye has been obtained from the flowers.

photograph by Ted Van Bruggen

Other common names: large-flowered everlasting, cottonweed, lady-never-fade, silver button, moonshine, silver leaf, Indian posy, ladies' tobacco, life everlasting, none-so-pretty, immortelle (Quebec)

Anaphalis: ancient Greek name for a similar plant; also a near-anagram of *Gnaphalium*

Margaritacea: meaning "pearly"

Daisy family: Asteraceae (Compositae)

Found throughout the tallgrass prairie as well as east and west to both coasts, north to Newfoundland, and across to Alaska. At least four varieties are found in areas ranging from slightly moist to mostly dry soils, in sand and gravel along streams, and on dry, open slopes up to subalpine areas. Several varieties are found farther south in mountain areas and in Europe and Asia. Blooms July to October.

Individual erect, cottony stems of common pearly everlasting grow to 3 feet tall. Narrow, alternate, sessile leaves up to 5 inches long are scattered along the upright stem. Leaves may be gray-green to woolly-white above but are almost always woolly-white beneath.

Flower heads are on short stalks in a flat-topped cluster at the top of the stem. The globular flowers are actually white, petal-like, blunt, dry bracts that are arranged in a tight series around a yellow center of stamens (in the male flowers). Each flower can be up to ⅓ inch across and ¼ inch high.

The male and female flowers are found on separate plants, similar to the genus *Antennaria* (which includes pussytoes). Some authorities, however, list male and female flowers as occurring separately on the same plant.

As one of the most showy of flowering plants, this conspicuous plant stands out in any natural setting. The dry strawlike bracts give the plant the appearance of flowering for most of the summer and fall. This characteristic has made it useful for cut flower arrangements that may last for several months.

No other specific uses by American Indians or pioneers are known.

This genus has approximately 30 species, and it has been used for hardy border plantings in landscaping. A related species from Asia that has yellow flowers is also sometimes used in landscape plantings.

Related species of cudweeds are sometimes considered weeds, but they can be easily controlled by cultivation.

photograph by Sylvan T. Runkel

Other common names: golden cassia, large-flowered sensitive pea, prairie senna pea, wild sensitive plant

Chamaecrista: from Greek, meaning "low crest"

Fasciculata: meaning "of bundles"

Legume family: Fabaceae (Leguminosae)

Found throughout the western portion of the tallgrass prairie on dry or sandy soils, especially on roadsides or disturbed sites. In prairies, it may be found on dry ridges or at a disturbed margin. It is also found at woodland edges and in low, sandy areas along streams. This annual thrives in full sunlight. Blooming time is July through September.

Partridge pea is a showy annual wildflower. Although it can grow to a height of over 2 feet, it usually is shorter. The stem, which may be smooth or finely hairy, may branch once.

Leaves are pinnately compound and occur alternately along the stem. Each leaf may have 15 pairs of leaflets that are oval and sessile (without petioles). The leaf resembles that of the locust tree, which is in the same family. Each leaflet is tipped with a tiny bristle. These leaflets fold along the midrib when touched. (This characteristic gave rise to the word *sensitive* in some of the common names.) The leaves fold in this manner at night and reopen during daylight.

The flowers, which ordinarily are canary yellow, are on slender stalks that arise from the upper leaf axils. Flowers are showy and rather large, usually an inch or more across. The five petals are unequal; each has a somewhat different shape and orientation. The lower petal and one lateral petal are largest; the upper petal is attached inside the others. There are five rather long sepals and 10 unequal stamens—6 have purple anthers, the remainder are yellow and rather inconspicuous.

The fruit, a hairy, flat pod, is up to 2 inches long and ¼ inch wide. When mature, the pod splits open, throwing the dozen or so small brown seeds some distance from the parent plant. The seeds are unusually viable and will form large aggressive populations that spread farther each year.

Medicinal uses of partridge pea by American Indians and pioneers are not known, but Old World medicine included products from related species. The drug senna comes from several species of *Chamaecrista* that are native to Egypt and Arabia.

Although the foliage of partridge pea is somewhat toxic to livestock, white-tailed deer browse on it. The seeds are readily eaten by bobwhite quail, greater and lesser prairie chickens, and kangaroo rats.

C. nictitans, a southern species, has small flowers and short pedicels.

photograph by Tomma Lou Maas

Other common names: woundwort, common woundwort, marsh woundwort, clown's woundwort

Stachys: from Greek, meaning "an ear of wheat or spike," referring to the terminal raceme

Palustris: meaning "of marshes"

Mint family: Lamiaceae (Labiatae)

Found in low prairies in the Upper Midwest. This perennial mint is a common member of the lowland prairie flora. Blooms from July through August.

Hedge nettle has the typical square mint stem. Growing to 2 feet tall, the stem is hairy and is usually unbranched. Leaves are opposite and stalkless. They taper abruptly toward the base. The leaves are pubescent beneath and hairy above and have distinctly toothed margins.

The flowers, which are rose-purple with a mottling of darker and lighter tones, occur on an elongate, tapering inflorescence. Individual flowers, approximately ½ inch long, have a large, three-lobed lower lip that is much longer than the arching upper lip. The downy calyx has sharp teeth that persist after maturity.

The dark brown ovary is deeply four-lobed and oval-shaped. Reproduction may be by seeds or by creeping rootstocks bearing subterranean stolons that terminate in tubers. Occasionally, stands of hedge nettle become very dense because of this method of spreading.

Early settlers used parts of this plant as a nauseant, an expectorant, an antihysteric, and a vulnerary (a substance that promotes healing of wounds). The Chippewa used it as a colic medicine. Medicinally, this species is thought to be the most important of the nearly 200 species in the genus.

The tubers of the hedge nettle have been boiled, dried, or made into bread for human consumption. An Asiatic species has been cultivated, and its tubers have been sold as Chinese artichokes.

Marsh hedge nettle (*S. tenuifolia*) is another common member of the moist-prairie flora that occurs at the edges of potholes. It closely resembles the hedge nettle, but its lower leaves are stalked and its spike has greater spacing between the flowers. A leaf tea made from this species was alleged to cure the common cold.

Because of their ability to survive in disturbed ground and because of their stoloniferous habit, the hedge nettles can become troublesome weeds. However, they are attractive and, in their proper habitat, interesting members of the prairie flora.

photograph by Ted Van Bruggen

Other common names: blackroot, Bowman's root, Culver's physic, high veronica, tall speedwell

Veronicastrum: named in honor of St. Veronica

Virginicum: meaning "of Virginia"

Snapdragon family: Scrophulariaceae

Found throughout the tallgrass prairie and elsewhere, especially on rich, moist soils. Blooms from July to late August.

This tall, graceful plant grows erect, from 2 to 7 feet tall. The stout, smooth stems may be somewhat branched at the top.

Its mostly horizontal, perennial root system is scarred on the top from past growth. An extensive network of fibrous rootlets grows from this branched root.

The leaves can be up to 6 inches long and 1 inch wide. They are slender ovals with pointed tips. Leaves, each on a short petiole, occur mostly in whorls of three to nine. The margins are notched with fine, sharp teeth. Leaf surfaces are generally smooth but are sometimes slightly hairy beneath, especially along the veins.

Flowers occur on slender, spikelike flower heads that are usually 3 to 9 inches long. There are one to nine flower heads per stem. Each flower is carried on a short stalk that is more or less at right angles to the main flower head stalk. These tiny, tubelike flowers, about ¼ inch long, are spread into four lobes that are shorter than the tube. The upper lobe tends to be wider than the others; the lower lobe tends to be the narrowest.

The fruit is two-celled. Each cell contains many tiny, black, roundish seeds that show net veining when they are examined closely.

The root was once used as a cathartic by early settlers, hence, the common name Culver's physic. It was often combined with other medicines. An infusion of the dried root was used cautiously for a sluggish liver. (One teaspoon of dried root steeped in 1 cup of boiling water for 30 minutes equaled one dose.) Fresh root was a drastic purge and abortivant, but its action was uncertain and severe.

Other uses of the root were as a stomach tonic, a laxative, an antiperiodic, a hepatic, and a cholagogue. It was also used to treat dyspepsia, torpidity of the liver, debilitated conditions of the digestive tract, typhoid, intermittent fever, diarrhea, and "summer bilious fevers."

The Seneca made a tea of the root for use as a mild laxative. Roots were gathered and stored at least a year before they were used. The root helped to promote vomiting. Taking a decoction of the root for a month was once considered a cure for venereal disease. For the Menomini, Culver's root served as a strong physic, a reviver, and as a means of purification when they had been defiled by the touch of a bereaved person. The Meskwaki used the root to treat constipation, to dissolve kidney stones, to make ague tea, and to treat women who were weak from labor.

photograph by LeRoy G. Pratt

Other common names: night willow-herb, large rampion, tree-primrose, king's cure-all, scurvish

Oenothera: a name used by Theophrastus for a species of *Epilobium,* another genus in this family. It also is Greek for "wine scented," referring to the scent of the flowers or to the fact that the roots were once used for wine.

Biennis: meaning "biennial," for its characteristic of living two years

Evening primrose family: Onagraceae

Found on most Midwest prairies on the dry ridges and gravelly or sandy areas. It also grows on roadsides, old fields, and waste areas. Blooming is from July through September.

During the first year, this plant appears as a coarse, flattened rosette of elongate leaves and strong, fleshy roots. In the second year, a stout stem develops that may reach a height of 6 feet, but normally it is less than 4 feet tall.

Leaves are alternate, sessile, light green, elliptic to lance-shaped, and up to 6 inches long. Lower portions of the stem are often tinged red to purple, as are parts of the older leaves, though there is great variation in this.

Bright yellow flowers up to 2 inches across have four notched petals and eight stamens. The stigma is prominently four-lobed. Each blossom lasts only about a day, opening abruptly in late afternoon to dusk. Because the flowers open at dusk, pollination is mainly accomplished by night-flying moths, but there is also some pollination by bees. New blooms continue to appear until frost.

The fruiting capsules, which are up to 1½ inches long, grow erect. There may be more than 50 capsules clustered along the upper stem. Seeds are angled and grow in two or more rows. Seeds are released over a considerable length of time.

Evening primrose has been used as a poultice. After the entire plant had been dried, a cold infusion was prepared and used to treat whooping cough, hiccoughs, and asthma. This infusion also served as an astringent and a sedative. Salves for the control of skin diseases were also prepared from this plant.

Seeds were used as a food by the Mohave. The first-year roots, gathered and dried, were an important food source for native Americans. (The second-year roots become woody and tough.) After this plant was introduced to Europe from North America in the early 1600s, its roots were eaten and the young shoots were used for salads.

The evening primrose does well in cultivated gardens that are in open sunlight.

Other species that occur on prairies in the tallgrass biome are *O. rhombipetela,* with rhomboid petals (found in sandy places); *O. laciniata,* with sinuate-pinnatifid leaves; *O. serrulata,* with a disklike stigma and narrow, serrate leaves; and *O. speciosa,* with white flowers. Identification is complicated because some species have a tendency to hybridize.

photograph by LeRoy G. Pratt

Other common names: bee balm, wild bergamot

Monarda: in honor of a Spanish physician and botanist, Nicolas Monardes, who wrote widely in the 16th century about medicinal and otherwise useful plants of the New World

Fistulosa: from Latin, meaning "like a reed or pipe," in reference to individual flowers

Mint family: Lamiaceae (Labiatae)

Found throughout the eastern and northeastern United States and the central tallgrass prairie, often on rich, moist soils. Commonly found along the edges of woods and on roadsides as well as in old pastures. Flowers July to September.

The square stem, a typical characteristic of the mint family, is sturdy and grows erect to about 5 feet tall. It is usually branched and somewhat hairy toward the top.

The leaves, on short petioles, are opposite; each pair is at right angles to the adjacent pair. Individual leaves are somewhat oval in shape but narrowed and pointed toward the tip. Margins are unevenly toothed.

Both leaves and stem have a minty aroma and a gray-green color that may be tinged with purple. These characteristics are typical of the mints. The aroma lasts into the winter, long after the foliage has died.

The perennial root system is a clump of fibrous rootlets and rhizomes.

Individual flowers are slender pink to lavender tubes, each with a distinct lip or lobe. These inch-long tubes cluster together in dense but ragged heads that may be 1½ inches across. Stamens protrude from the tubes, adding to the ragged appearance.

The Winnebago boiled the leaves to secure an oil they used to treat pimples and similar skin eruptions. The Blackfoot applied boiled leaves for the same purpose. The Meskwaki used the plant in a mixture to cure colds. Navajos and early pioneers made a tea of horsemint to treat fevers, sore throat, colds, and headache. Other American Indians used a warm liquid from the boiled leaves to bathe a patient suffering from chills. The aromatic dried herb was boiled to produce vapors for bronchial ailments. A tea of the roots was used to treat stomach disorders.

Because its plants have small glands that secrete characteristic aromatic and volatile oils, the mint family has furnished humans with many herbs and flavorings. Among those still being used are marjoram, rosemary, peppermint, spearmint, horehound, thyme, sage, lavender, catnip, hyssop, and pennyroyal.

At least one other *Monarda* species is native to the central tallgrass prairie area. *M. punctata* is shorter than horsemint and has yellow flowers spotted with purple dots. Although it is a native of the eastern United States, *M. didyma,* called oswega tea, has escaped from garden plantings in the central prairie area. Its beautiful crimson flower may brighten the countryside, especially along streams, in late summer.

photograph by Randall A. Maas

Other common names: basil, mountain thyme, pennyroyal, prairie hyssop

Pycnanthemum: from the Greek *pycnos,* meaning "dense," and *anthemon,* meaning "a flower," from the compact flower head

Virginianum: meaning "of Virginia"

Mint family: Lamiaceae (Labiatae)

Found in wet to dry prairies and open spaces throughout the tallgrass prairie and areas to the north and east. Blooms July through September.

This stout, erect perennial tends to be multibranched toward the top. As is typical of the mints, the stem is four-angled and covered with a whitish bloom. The sides are smooth, but the angles have a covering of fine hairs. The plant usually grows 2 to 3 feet tall and is covered with many leaves.

Mountain mint and most of the other species in this genus are very fragrant. When crushed, the leaves have a strong minty odor. The opposite leaves are narrow and lance-shaped, rounded at the base and pointed at the tip. The margins and upper surface are smooth and the underside may be hairy. Main leaves are as long as 2 inches and less than ½ inch wide. Short, leafy branches often arise from the axils of upper leaves.

Tiny, mint-type flowers have a lower lip with three rounded lobes and an upper lip that may have a slight notch at the tip. The upper lip is white; the lower is often spotted with purple.

The flowers are arranged in numerous, dense, headlike clusters that are about ¼ inch across. The clusters arise from axils of the upper leaves and at the stem tip. Only a few are in bloom at one time.

Seeds are tiny, with a smooth to rough surface.

The Meskwaki used mountain mint as a medicine (unspecified) and for baiting mink traps. The Potawatomi considered it one of the best tonics for a rundown condition. A tea made from the leaves was preferred, but roots were also used.

Early settlers once used a mountain mint poultice on dog and other animal bites as a rabies preventative. A tea brewed from the leaves served as a general tonic and as a treatment for mild indigestion and for the chills and fever of ague.

The leaves have been used as a seasoning in cooking.

About 17 species in this genus are native to North America.

photograph by LeRoy G. Pratt

Other common names: gayfeather, button snakeroot, tall gayfeather

Liatris: derivation unknown

Aspera: from Latin, meaning "rough" or "harsh," from the coarse nature of the leaves

Daisy family: Asteraceae (Compositae)

Found on dry, often sandy, soil throughout most of the tallgrass prairie biome. Occasionally it is found in dense populations, especially following a prairie fire. Flowers from July into September.

This perennial grows from 1 to 4 feet tall from a rounded, fiber-covered corm. The stem is downy and bears rough, narrow, linear leaves that are ½ to ¾ inch wide. The leaves are alternate and often have resinous dots on them.

The inflorescence is a long raceme composed of up to 150 heads. Each individual head consists of up to 40 flowers and has numerous bracts. The flowers are rose-purple, but occasionally white forms appear. Prior to opening, the flower head has a buttonlike appearance, hence, one of its common names.

The seed is an achene, ¼ inch long, with a longer attachment of hairs (pappus). This plant reproduces by rhizome or by seed.

Most members of the genus *Liatris* were used extensively by early Americans. The bulbs were given to horses to increase their endurance, and they were utilized by humans as a diuretic, a stimulant, a diaphoretic, and an emmenagogue. *L. pycnostachya* was used to treat gonorrhea, sore throat, and diseases of the kidneys. Corms of *L. aspera* were once dug and stored for winter meals, and a tea was made from the leaves to treat snakebites and stomach aches.

This attractive genus has gained little favor with wildflower garden enthusiasts, although it richly deserves ornamental uses.

There are approximately 25 species of this genus in North America. Many are similar in appearance and some hybridize to produce intermediate forms.

In addition to *L. aspera* and *L. pycnostachya,* the most frequently encountered species, the following occur in the tallgrass biome: *L. cylindracea,* a northeastern species, and *L. squarrosa,* a southeastern species, have heads of 15 to 60 flowers. *L. ligulistylis* has straplike styles and large flower heads. *L. punctata,* a western species, has long, leafy bracts and translucent dots on the leaves. *L. spicata,* an eastern species, has very many narrow leaves. *L. angustifolia* is a southwestern species.

The sight of the native prairie at the height of the blooming season for blazing star is a never-to-be-forgotten experience.

photograph by John Schwegman

Other common names: old witchgrass, tickle grass, mousseline, tumblegrass

Panicum: from Latin *panus,* probably meaning "an ear of millet"

Capillare: from Latin, meaning "hairlike"

Grass family: Poaceae (Gramineae)

Found throughout the tallgrass and mixed-grass prairie, especially where the prairie is in a poor or degraded condition. Witchgrass is often found on roadsides and sandy soils. It is seldom found in other than scattered stands and is rare in vigorous, thriving prairies. In the original native prairie, it was found only in naturally disturbed sites, such as along animal trails or at the edges of buffalo wallows. Blooming time is July to September.

This weedy, warm season annual grows 1 to 2½ feet tall in small tufts or bunches. It is usually branched from the base, with stems that are generally erect but sometimes have a tendency to spread.

The stems and leaf sheaths are quite hairy, giving the plant a woolly appearance. As in some other panicums, a nest of hair is found where each leaf joins the stem. Even the leaf blades have scattered hairs on both surfaces. Leaf blades are less than 1 inch wide—often considerably less—and may reach 10 inches long.

The entire seed head is about one-third of the total plant height and is about half as wide as it is long. The seed head has a loose, open appearance because of its threadlike branches (from which the species name is derived). At the base of each branch of the seed head is a prominent tuft of hairs. The single-flowered spikelets are usually about ⅛ inch long. The first sharply pointed glume is about one-third as long as the second glume.

The small, rounded seeds are a shiny grayish brown in color. Reproduction is by seed.

This grass is rather undistinguished until early fall, when the seed heads open to their full size and mature to a purplish color. The entire seed head often breaks loose from the plant and rolls in the wind like a miniature "tumbleweed."

The seed provides food for songbirds.

Witchgrass is not good for grazing except in the early stage of growth before the seeds develop. It is nearly worthless as standing forage or hay. It is often a nuisance on cultivated land, where it competes vigorously with new seedlings.

A related species provides millet-like grain for American Indians of the Southwest.

photograph by Ted Van Bruggen

Other common names: catfoot, sweet balsam, sweet everlasting, sweet life, white balsam, rabbit tobacco, cottonweed, silver leaf

Gnaphalium: from Greek *gnaphalium,* meaning "a lock of wool," in reference to the woolly character of the plant

Obtusifolium: from Latin *obtus,* meaning "dull or blunt," and *folium,* meaning "leaf," in reference to the rounded leaf tips

Daisy family: Asteraceae (Compositae)

Found in dry, open places throughout the Midwest prairie region. Blooms from July through September.

Cudweed is a biennial that has a first-year rosette. The erect, leafy stems are from 8 inches to 3 feet high and may be branched toward the top. White woolly hairs cover the stems. It is mildly fragrant when bruised.

The sessile leaves are narrowed toward the base and have blunt tips. The leaf base does not extend downward as it does in some other species of *Gnaphalium.* The leaves are densely whitish woolly beneath, smooth and dark green above. They have smooth or wavy leaf margins. Leaves are 1 to 3 inches long and ⅙ to ⅓ inch wide.

Clusters of one to five small white flower heads, ¼ inch long, are made up of tiny, tubular, threadlike disk flowers that resemble tufts of wool. Bracts are white or tinged with brown.

The tiny, wedge-shaped seeds are about ⅓ to ½ inch long. The seed has a tuft of hairs at one end.

When chewed, cudweed served as an astringent for sores in the mouth and for sore throats. It was also chewed to increase the flow of saliva. Because of this quality, it was given to cattle that had lost the ability to ruminate (lost their cud); this is supposedly why it is called cudweed.

A cold infusion was used for diarrhea, for dysentery, and sometimes for the treatment of worms. Fresh juice of the plant was a treatment for venereal disease, tumors, and ulcers.

A hot fermentation of an extract was useful in treating wounds, sprains, and bruises. This species was boiled together with horsemint (*Monarda fistulosa*) and used as a tea for treating delirium. A hot decoction was considered good for the lungs and chest, for easing pain, and for inducing sweating in the treatment of the early stages of fever.

To revive consciousness, the smoke from burning leaves was blown into the nostrils of one who had fainted. This procedure was also used to bring back loss of memory. A pillow filled with dried flowers was used to quiet coughing. Plants laid in drawers and wardrobes kept away moths.

Pliny recommended that the juice of *Gnaphalium* (probably *G. uliginosum*) be taken in wine and milk as a "sovereign" remedy against mumps and "quinsey" (sore throat). It was thought that, once treated, one would never have the disease again.

When one of the family of a Menomini died, his spirit or ghost was supposed to come back to trouble the living with bad luck, nightmares, and so forth. Fumigating the premises with a smudge of *Gnaphalium* species displeased the ghost and caused it to leave, never to return.

photograph by Dean Roosa

Other common names: side oats, grama grass, mesquite grass, tall grama grass

Bouteloua: named for Claudio Boutelou, a 19th century Spanish writer and botanist

Curtipendula: from Latin, meaning "short-hanging"

Grass family: Poaceae (Gramineae)

Found in drier areas of the tallgrass prairie (such as shallow ridges, rocky areas, steep slopes, and well-drained uplands) and westward throughout the Great Plains. It does not tolerate shading by tall grasses. Blooms July to September.

The smooth, erect stems of this unusual perennial grow unbranched to heights of 3 feet. Stems rise from a dense root system of short, slender, scaly rhizomes. This tends to give the plant a bunchy appearance, even though it is a sod-forming grass.

Leaf blades are only about ⅛ inch wide but range from 4 to 12 inches long. They are generally rough on the upper side and are sometimes hairy beneath. They narrow toward a dried tip that is shaped like a flattened bristle. Leaves normally have widely spaced, stiff hairs projecting from their margins.

The ligule (the collar at the junction of the blade and sheath) is a zone of short hairs. The sheaths are longer than the internodes of the stem. These sheaths may be lightly hairy toward the top but otherwise are nearly smooth.

The lower leaves tend to turn whitish and to curl when they are dry. The green leaves frequently have dark spots, as if they were diseased. During late summer and fall, the entire plant takes on a reddish cast.

The purplish seed heads are 4 to 12 inches long and consist of 10 to 50 spikelets that droop from one side of the seedstalk. Although all spikelets hang to one side, they are actually attached around the stem. Each spikelet is about ⅓ inch long and contains three to six individual flowers.

The fruits are small, oatlike seeds. Approximately 500,000 seeds are needed to make up a pound. The oatlike appearance of the seeds and the unusual positioning of the spikelets give rise to the descriptive "side oats" portion of this plant's common name.

Side oats grama grass is a palatable, nutritious forage grain with wide use for grazing and as a constituent of prairie hay. A commercial variety has been developed for forage and hay. When planted for pasture, it responds well to nitrogen fertilizer.

This plant is included in most prairie plantings, and it is excellent for conservation practices.

There are about 40 *Bouteloua* species, half of which are found in the United States. All except side oats grama grass are western species. Two other grama grasses—*B. gracilis,* blue grama, and *B. hirsuta,* hairy grama—are sometimes seen in the drier western edge of the tallgrass prairie. These are easily identified by their inflorescence or seed head, which resembles a human eyebrow.

photograph by John Schwegman

Other common names: roundhead bushclover, dusty clover

Lespedeza: named after Cespedez, the Spanish governor of east Florida in the late 18th century, although the name was misspelled as Lespedeza

Capitata: from Latin, meaning "in heads," referring to the seed heads

Legume family: Fabaceae (Leguminosae)

Found on dry prairie and open woodland soils in the Midwest and east of the Great Plains. Blooms July to September.

Roundhead lespedeza is a native perennial legume that grows 2 to 4 feet high. The entire plant is covered with a fine, silvery hair.

The leaves occur alternately along the erect stems. They have three leaflets of medium to narrow elliptic shape.

The creamy white legume-type flowers are small. They occur in tight heads that are round or knob-shaped and ½ to 1½ inches in diameter. The flower heads are found growing close to the erect stems and are mostly near the top of the stems.

The Comanche made a beverage from the leaves of roundhead lespedeza. The Dakota, the Omaha, and the Ponca used the stems for a moxa in cases of neuralgia and rheumatism. The small stems were cut in short pieces and attached to the skin by moistening one end with the tongue; the other end was set on fire and allowed to burn down to the skin.

The root of roundhead lespedeza was considered an antidote to poisons that had been swallowed. The exact method of treatment was not specified.

At one time, this plant was being studied by French scientists for possible medicinal uses.

This plant provides a nutritious high-protein forage for wild, grazing animals. Ranchers and livestockmen consider it to be a valuable and nutritious range plant. The seeds are eaten by songbirds, gamebirds, and other wildlife.

The related Korean lespedeza, which originated in Asia, has been planted widely in this country for pasture and for a ground cover on poor and eroded soils. It is much smaller than our native lespedezas, but it is able to grow on poor and tight soils. It furnishes not only pasture forage but also seeds, which are eaten by quail, pheasants, grouse, and many kinds of songbirds.

Prairie bushclover (*L. leptostachya*) is somewhat similar to roundhead lespedeza, but it is very rare and restricted in its range. It occurs in Iowa, southern Minnesota, southern Wisconsin, and northern Illinois.

photograph by John Schwegman

Other common names: western false boneset

Kuhnia: named for Dr. Adam Kuhn, who carried the living plant to Linnaeus

Eupatorioides: from its resemblance to *Eupatorium,* another genus in the same family

Daisy family: Asteraceae (Compositae)

Found throughout the United States in drier prairies and plains and in open, rocky woods. The two varieties of this species usually occur as scattered plants, and they are seldom abundant. Blooms through the fall into October.

Growth of a few to many stems occurs from the enlarged crown of the deep, woody taproot. This perennial may reach a height of 2 to 3 feet and have a bushy appearance when numerous stems are present. The plant usually has a whitish appearance.

Alternate, lance-shaped leaves are minutely pubescent. They have prominent raised veins on the underside, and their margins vary from shallow-toothed to entire. The upper leaves are sessile, while the lower ones have short petioles. All are dotted with resin glands. Real boneset (*Eupatorium perfoliatum*) looks very much like *Kuhnia* except that the leaves are opposite, with the bases united around the stem.

The small, numerous, white or yellowish flowers occur in clusters at the tips of branches in the form of flat-topped heads. The real resemblance to boneset is from the flowers, which consist of only tubular florets. Flowers are normally less than ½ inch long.

As the fruits mature, attached hairlike structures called plumules become conspicuous. These aid in wind dispersal of the seed, which is the plant's usual mode of dissemination, since it does not spread by rhizomes.

Some sources said that false boneset was used by Great Plains Indians for an application to reduce swelling. Its bitter taste restricted its use as a food plant or medicine.

Young plants are palatable to livestock, but grazing causes a marked decrease in the abundance of the plant.

Most dry prairies support a population of false boneset. Its flowers add color and interest to the last stages of the prairie year. The dried seed head has also been used as an attractive addition to winter bouquets.

photograph by Ted Van Bruggen

Other common names: western ironweed

Vernonia: named for William Vernon, an English botanist

Fasciculata: meaning "bunched," referring to the cluster of stems that emerge together

Daisy family: Asteraceae (Compositae)

Found throughout the tallgrass prairie biome in wet areas and on roadsides as well as in marshes. Blooms July to September.

The cluster of often reddish stems grows to over 6 feet high. The many glabrous, linear or lance-shaped leaves are sessile or have short stalks; they have sharp teeth on the margins. Small pits dot the undersides of the deep green leaves.

The deep purple flower heads form a spreading inflorescence of 20 to 30 symmetrical florets that make up a cyme. The cyme, which may reach 6 inches across, appears in late summer.

Seeds are dark, oblong, and prominently ribbed. Reproduction occurs by seeds or by rhizomes.

Due to its tough, fibrous nature and bitter taste, ironweed has been of apparently little or no use as a medicinal plant or as a food for wildlife. It may become a pest in prairie pastures and is a sign of overgrazing. Since it is considered unpalatable, it is usually undisturbed while other plants are grazed.

The name ironweed comes from the toughness of the plant. Beekeepers know it as a good nectar producer.

There are at least five species of *Vernonia* found in the tallgrass prairie biome. Other plants of the genus are *V. altissima,* tall ironweed, which has downy leaves and hairy achenes; *V. missurica,* Missouri ironweed, which has tomentose lower leaf surfaces; *V. baldwini,* which has shorter achenes and fewer flowers in the head; and *V. crinita,* which has long, willowlike leaves and occurs in the southern portion of the tallgrass biome. Many hybrids form where species overlap, making precise identification difficult.

Many people think the ironweeds are the loveliest of the late summer and fall blooming prairie plants. They add a splash of intense purple color to the otherwise subdued autumn prairie landscape.

photograph by LeRoy G. Pratt

Other common names: wood grass, yellow Indian grass, bushy bluestem, wild oatgrass

Sorghastrum: from Greek, meaning generally "a poor imitation of sorghum," for its resemblance to the sorghum genus

Nutans: from Latin, meaning generally "nodding" or "swaying"

Grass family: Poaceae (Gramineae)

Found throughout the prairie area, especially in conjunction with the bluestems. It generally favors more mesic sites than those preferred by big bluestem. Growth begins in late April or early May. Flowering occurs in late July and August.

This vigorous perennial grows 2½ to 6 feet tall, sometimes as much as 8 feet. Early growth resembles that of big bluestem, but it is generally a lighter green.

Stems are stout, erect, and unbranched. They are smooth except for a covering of soft, silky, golden hairs at the nodes. The extensive root system produces short, scaly rhizomes as one means of reproduction.

The leaves, usually less than 2 feet long, are rather stiff and straight. Spreading from the stem at about a 45° angle, the leaves are about ¼ to more than ½ inch wide, narrowing where they join the sheath. Leaves are rough to the touch and have a whitish bloom. Leaf sheaths tend to be smooth, although the lower ones may be slightly hairy.

The ligule (the collar formed by the joining of the leaf blade and the leaf sheath) usually extends less than ⅛ inch upward. It forms a clawlike projection, a characteristic of the species that is sometimes referred to as being "similar to a rifle sight."

Conspicuous yellow anthers give the 4- to 12-inch-long flower heads a yellowish appearance. Within the head are numerous individual branches 2 to 4 inches long. Each branch is erect, becoming nodding at the tip as the seeds mature.

Spikelets develop along each branch. Fertile spikelets ¼ to ⅓ inch long have two outer glumes. These glossy bronze-colored glumes have fawn-colored hairs. The fertile spikelet is tipped with an awn about three times as long as the spikelet itself. The awn has a slight bend; it is closely spiraled from the base to the bend and loosely twisted toward the tip. Opposite each fertile spikelet is a rudimentary one, often just a tiny, hairy stalk.

The seed matures from September to frost or even later. It requires about 175,000 spikelets to make a pound of seed.

A common constituent of prairie hay, Indian grass is a nutritious forage. It is readily eaten by livestock either as dry prairie hay or as green forage.

Sometimes Indian grass is used as a border for wildflower gardens because of its showy appearance.

photograph by John Schwegman

Other common names: cudweed, mugwort, sagebrush, dark-leaved mugwort, sagewort, western mugwort, western sage, white sage, wormwood

Artemisia: an ancient name for this genus; in memory of Artemisia, wife of Mausolus, king of ancient Caria in southwest Asia Minor on the Mediterranean Sea. (The elaborate tomb she built for her husband gave us the term *mausoleum*.)

Ludoviciana: from a form of Latin meaning "of Louisiana," probably "of St. Louis" in this case. (There are at least six varieties of this species.)

Daisy family: Asteraceae (Compositae)

Found throughout the tallgrass prairie and beyond, especially in disturbed areas along roads and railways. Prairie sage prefers drier areas on rocky, sandy, or gravelly loam soils. Blooms August through September.

These highly variable and aggressive weedy plants produce a few to many clustered stems that grow up to 40 inches tall. The stems are multibranched and are thickly covered by a fuzzy mat of grayish hairs. The perennial, slender, cordlike rhizomes form a dense mat near the soil surface.

Alternate leaves vary from thin, pointed ovals that are almost grasslike to broad ovals that are deeply divided into narrow segments. These leaves, perhaps 3 or more inches long, are covered beneath with a felt-like mass of whitish hairs. The foliage has a bitter taste and a strong odor.

Numerous small heads, each about ⅛ inch across, are borne in the upper leaf axils and at the ends of the upper branches. Each flower head is made up of numerous tubular florets. They are an inconspicuous whitish green color.

American Indians used this species for medicinal purposes and for religious ceremonies. Dakotas liked to begin ceremonies with sage to drive away any evil influences. Some tribes believed that a person who had carelessly broken a taboo or touched a sacred object could be restored to good standing by bathing in water with prairie sage in it. The Omaha used it as a bed for sacred smoking pipes. Before a body was carried into the church for a funeral, pioneers burned the tops of prairie sage in a small fire in front of the steps to provide incense.

Arikara women took an infusion of *A. ludoviciana* to control profuse menstruation and to relieve pain. Some American Indians used it for stomach troubles. A tea was made from the leaves for treating tonsillitis, sore throat, and genital troubles.

The Meskwaki and the Potawatomi had separate names for the plant but both meant "mosquito smoke." They burned the plant and made a smudge to drive away mosquitos and insects. They also used it as a poultice on long-standing sores.

Sage seasoning is not derived from this plant; it comes from a member of the mint family.

Tall wormwood, *A. caudata,* is common in the tallgrass prairie. It prefers the sands of dry beaches and shorelines.

photograph by Sylvan T. Runkel

Other common names: roadside thistle

Cirsium: name derived from Cirsion, used by Dioscorides and derived from the Greek *cirsos,* meaning "a swollen vein," for which the thistle was once considered a remedy

Altissimum: from Latin, generally meaning "especially tall"

Daisy family: Asteraceae (Compositae)

Found on rich soils of the tallgrass prairie and to the east and south. Flowers August and September.

Growing from 3 to 12 feet tall (usually less than 12), this plant has most of the characteristics of typical thistles. The stem may be branched. The deep taproot generally is biennial, but sometimes it is perennial.

The alternate, deep green leaves of tall thistle grow to 12 inches long. They are not lobed except perhaps for a few toward the base, although each of the coarse teeth on the leaf margin ends in a sharp spine. (Most thistles, including the native field thistles *C. discolor* and *C. flodmani* as well as the alien bull thistle, *C. vulgare,* have deeply-lobed leaves.)

The undersides of the leaves of tall thistle, as well as the other species mentioned, are a woolly whitish color. However, Hill's thistle (*C. hillii*), a frequent prairie inhabitant that is only 1 to 2 feet high, has leaves that are green on both sides.

The small uppermost leaves of tall thistle and field thistle occur immediately below the flower and rise to surround its base.

Typical, thistle-type flower heads appear in August and September. Those of the tall thistle are a rosy purple, rarely white. They measure 1½ to 2 inches high, with about 1 inch being the green cuplike base formed by the bracts. Each of the outer bracts is tipped with a bristle pointing outward. A mass of thin tubular flowers extends from this "cup" to form the flower head that is distinctive of the thistles.

The flattened, oblong-shaped seeds have a plume of soft bristles.

Young leaves, young stems, and roots of this and other thistles may be used in salads, as cooking greens, or as cooked vegetables. The roots of the first-year plants (those without stems) are a good source of food when conventional foods are lacking. The thistle and the artichoke are related; if properly used, both have been considered edible.

The goldfinch is sometimes known as the thistle bird because of its preference for thistle down as nest-building material.

Thistles have been known and respected for centuries. In Scotland, the thistle has a revered place in the history of the country. It was responsible for alerting the country's defenders when enemy attackers cried out as they stepped on the spiny thistles.

photograph by Ted Van Bruggen

Other common names: Wobsqua grass, blackbent, tall prairie grass, wild red top, thatch grass

Panicum: from Latin *panus,* probably meaning generally "an ear of millet"

Virgatum: from Latin, meaning generally "wandlike"

Grass family: Poaceae (Gramineae)

Found in favorable habitats throughout the United States, especially at the western edge of the tallgrass prairie and in the eastern Great Plains. It prefers the low, moist areas. Flowers from August to September.

This vigorous, sod-forming perennial often grows in dense colonies. The root system produces short, stout, scaly rhizomes that send up new shoots to form the dense sod of switchgrass colonies. Growth begins in late spring and continues through summer if moisture is adequate.

Its stout, erect, unbranched stems grow 3 to 6 feet tall, a little shorter than those of big bluestem and Indian grass, which may be growing in the same stand. Stems are green to purplish.

The leaf blades are generally 6 to 18 inches long and are ¼ to ½ inch wide, narrowing toward the sheath. The blade surfaces are smooth but the margins are rough.

The sheaths are smooth. Sheaths of the middle and lower leaves are longer than the internodes of the stem; those of the upper leaves are shorter than corresponding internodes.

The ligule, a collar formed where the leaf blade joins the sheath, is one of the species' distinguishing features. It is a tuft of hairs. A V-shaped zone of hairs extends from this tufted ligule onto the upper surface of the leaf blade.

A loose flower head takes up the top 6 to 20 inches of a stem. Individual lower branches of the head may be 4 to 10 inches long. Spikelets along the branches are ⅛ to ¼ inch long. The first glume of the spikelet is only one-third to two-thirds as long as the spikelet. The second glume is longer. Both glumes show three to five conspicuous veins. At flowering, the purple anthers give the head a purplish appearance.

Seeds mature in September. They are small and require nearly 400,000 per pound.

The genus, which contains about 500 species, is a relative of various millets. Millets are important food plants in parts of India and China, especially when rice is in short supply. Millet also was an important cereal crop of the Mediterranean region in ancient times.

Switchgrass was avoided by buffalo hunters when they cut up carcasses in the field. Its tiny spikes tended to stick into the meat — and sometimes in the throat of the consumer.

This grass has a way of creeping inside one's trouser legs, giving rise to numerous uncomplimentary local names.

Panicum species are important food sources for many kinds of birds and browsing animals. Domesticated varieties have been developed for improved forage.

photograph by Randall A. Maas

Other common names: rigid goldenrod, hard-leaved goldenrod

Solidago: from Latin *solidus* or *solidare*, meaning "to make whole" or "to strengthen," probably an allusion to the healing powers of the genus

Rigida: from its stiffly erect habit

Daisy family: Asteraceae (Compositae)

Found widely distributed in eastern and central United States on dry prairies, dry open woods, roadsides, and disturbed areas. It probably occurs in every prairie in the tallgrass biome. Like most members of the genus, it blooms late—August to October.

This coarse, erect perennial often occurs in clumps. The fibrous roots may penetrate the soil 5 feet, so it competes well with the dominant grass species.

The plant may grow to a height of over 3 feet—even 4 feet may be reached in the eastern portion of its range. The leaves and stem are usually hairy, giving the plant a distinctive pale green or grayish cast.

Leaves are alternate, with the lower ones long-petioled and oval. The upper leaves are smaller, sessile, and ovate to oblong; they slightly clasp the stem. All are sparsely toothed and are harsh and leathery. The lower leaves form a large basal rosette early in the season or sometimes in the previous fall, so the plant is discernible throughout the growing season.

The terminal inflorescence is bright yellow, more or less flat-topped to somewhat rounded, dense, and up to several inches across. The mass of tiny, golden flowers, individually about ⅓ inch long, combine to make a large, handsome spray.

Reproduction is by lateral shoots and by seeds.

Bee stings were once treated with a lotion made from the flowers of stiff goldenrod. Swollen throats were treated with a liquid made by boiling its leaves.

It is an invader that increases in grazed pastures because it is eaten only in the early stages of its growth.

A hardy species that is attractive in bloom, stiff goldenrod would complement a flower garden.

While this is an easily recognized species, goldenrods in general cannot be recommended to the amateur naturalist. Some species are distinctive, but many appear identical and are separated on the basis of minor characters. Professional taxonomists do not agree on species limits, and many goldenrods hybridize.

Goldenrods have been blamed for the allergic reaction of hay fever, but this lacks substantiation. Hay fever is mainly caused by the wind-blown pollen of ragweed, and goldenrods are primarily insect-pollinated.

photograph by John Schwegman

Other common names: northern dropseed, prairie dropseed, bunchgrass

Sporobolus: from Greek *spora,* meaning "seed," and *ballein,* meaning "to cast forth," in reference to the prompt dropping of its seeds when they reach maturity

Heterolepis: from Latin, meaning generally "with unequal glumes"

Grass family: Poaceae (Gramineae)

Found in open prairies, sometimes in almost solid stands. Common in dry, rocky areas. Flowering time is from August to October.

The rather stout, wiry stems of this warm season perennial grow erect to more than 3 feet tall. It forms rather graceful, fountain-like clumps that are 6 to 8 inches across at the base. The stems are pithy, and the foliage has a strong, noticeably grassy scent. In the winter, it bleaches white and tends to stand out among other grasses.

The slender, flat leaf blades are less than ⅛ inch across but are 8 to 20 inches long. Their narrow tips tend to be dry and curled inward. The margins and midribs are rough. Sheaths are hairy at the throat where the blade joins the sheath.

The seed head emerges from its sheath at flowering time. Shaped like a narrow cone, it generally reaches 3 to 12 inches long but is seldom more than 3 inches across. The seed head color varies from pinkish brown to grayish to blackish. Seed head branches are slightly spreading, erect, and close to the main seedstalks.

The single-flowered spikelets are about ⅛ inch long. Their first glume is about half as long as the second.

Tiny, roundish, nutlike seeds that are approximately 1/16 inch across have a hard, shiny coat. They shatter easily and may lie dormant for years before germinating under natural conditions.

The seed of dropseed is fragrant and tasty. The Kiowa parched the tiny grains and ground them into flour. It is also an important source of food for ground-feeding birds.

Sand dropseed (*S. cryptandrus*) is easily distinguished from dropseed by a conspicuous dense tuft of white hair at the base of the leaf blade and leading down the sheath. Sand dropseed was also frequently used by native Americans as food.

This genus includes over 35 native species. They are found mainly in the dry areas of the Southwest.

photograph by Richard F. Trump

Other common names: doghair grass, needle grass, tickle grass, white grass, wiregrass, poverty grass

Aristida: from Latin *arista,* meaning "a beard or awn"

Oligantha: from Latin, meaning "few-flowered"

Grass family: Poaceae (Gramineae)

Found on dry, open soils of the tallgrass prairie. It is also found in the Great Plains, but other species of the genus are more common to the west. It is probably the most frequently encountered *Aristida* in the tallgrass prairie biome. Blooms August to September.

This warm season annual grows in tufts, with stems 1 to 2 feet tall. It branches freely at the base and lower nodes. At maturity, it is tough and wiry, with a distinctive whitish color. The shallow root system is fine and fibrous.

Leaves are mostly basal and are usually less than 6 inches long. They are narrow, tapering to a fine point. The loose sheath of stem leaves tends to be longer or shorter than the stem internodes. The ligule (the collar where the blade joins the sheath) is small and hairy. Leaf blades are generally smooth but sometimes have a few hairs.

The loose seed head, which is usually 4 to 8 inches long, has few seeds. The lower spikelets along the seed stem are paired; the upper awns are solitary. Each spikelet has its own short stalk. Unlike most grasses, the first glume is longer than the second and tapers into an awn.

Attached to each seed are three divergent awns, each 1 to 2½ inches long. These awns are stiff and straight and are somewhat spiraled toward the base. In addition to aiding dispersal by attaching to the fur and hair of animals, the awns aid in wind-dispersal of the seeds in open country. The small seeds also often stick to clothing.

Since the mature awns can cause injury to livestock if they are eaten, prairie three awn is of little value for forage except before it flowers.

This species tends to increase with overgrazing of the prairie, but it does not compete well with thick stands of the better grasses. It is one of the most common invaders of overgrazed range lands.

It is food for rodents, but it is not important for birds.

Some 40 three awn species occur in North and Central America; none are of great importance economically. There is little reference of their utilization by humans.

photograph by Ted Van Bruggen

Other common names: beardgrass, blue joint, turkey foot

Andropogon: from Greek *andros,* meaning "man's," and *pogon,* meaning "beard," probably because of the hairy appearance given to the seed heads by the sterile glumes

Gerardi: for Louis Gerard, a French botanist of the late 1700s and early 1800s who first described this species in technical terms

Grass family: Poaceae (Gramineae)

Found from the Atlantic Ocean to the Rocky Mountains, most commonly through the tallgrass prairie regions of the Great Plains. Often the predominant species, it once covered thousands of square miles of eastern prairie in Iowa, Illinois, parts of Minnesota, and Missouri. Blooms August through September.

This coarse, leafy grass occurs in large clumps and forms a dense sod. Its growth usually begins in April and continues through the entire summer.

Big bluestem spreads by seeds and, slowly, by rhizomes. The root system of this perennial has coarse branches throughout the top couple of feet of soil and may extend to depths of 12 feet.

Plant stems grow to heights of 8 feet. Nodes tend to be bluish, giving rise to the name bluestem. Unlike most grasses, these stems are solid or pithy, not hollow. Some stems may fork toward the top, with each branch producing a seed head. Seed heads are produced from August until frost.

The leaves are green with a bluish cast and are sometimes tinged with red or purple, which gives them a mottled appearance. They hold their green color longer than most associated grasses, but they take on a reddish cast after frost. Leaves grow up to 2 feet long and are mostly ¼ to ½ inch wide.

The inflorescence usually divides into three branches, giving rise to the name turkey foot. Each part, usually 2 to 4 inches long, generally is bronze to purplish but may be green.

Along each stalk of the seed head, two opposite spikelets, one fertile and one sterile, are borne at each node. Each node carries a ring of tiny white hairs. The sterile spikelet is borne on a separate, short, flattened stalk (pedicel).

The Chippewa used big bluestem as medicine for indigestion and stomach pains. Roots, in a water decoction, were used for "stoppage of urine." The Omaha made a decoction of the lower leaf blades to treat general debility from an unknown cause. For fevers, a cut was made on the top of the head and bathed with this decoction. If a fever developed from a wound, the lower leaves were applied directly to the wound.

In *Uses of Plants by the Indians of the Missouri River Region,* Melvin Gilmore told of a woman (Ponka-sa) who, after being taught to knit, lost her needles and improvised a set from the stem of big bluestem.

The "king of native grasses," big bluestem was the main constituent of prairie hay. (The Omaha-Ponca name for big bluestem was *hade-zhide,* meaning "red hay.") Early settlers found that corn grew best where "big blue" grew. Most of the top corn land of the cornbelt once supported stands of big bluestem.

photograph by John Schwegman

Other common names: broom beardgrass, wiregrass, bunchgrass, prairie beardgrass, broom

Andropogon: from Greek *andros,* meaning "man's," and *pogon,* meaning "beard," probably because of the hairy appearance given to the seed heads by the sterile glumes

Scoparius: from a Latin word meaning "broomlike"

Grass family: Poaceae (Gramineae)

Found in association with its relative, big bluestem, but on lighter soils and as an intermediate between the tall grasses and the shorter grasses on the dry knolls. It is more common in the midgrass prairie of the Great Plains, especially in the famed Flint Hills regions of Kansas and Oklahoma, and north to the Canadian border. Blooms August to October.

This vigorous, long-lived species grows in clumps that are sometimes dense, sometimes loose. There is usually space between clumps, which is typical of a bunchgrass.

It is smaller than big bluestem, usually 1 to 3 feet tall, but it grows to 5 feet when conditions are ideal. Growth starts in April and continues through the season.

Basal shoots are usually flattened and are bluish green in color. The lower portions of the stems and the leaf sheaths are also somewhat flattened. Nodes of the stems are often bluish or purplish. Stems are stiff and hard, and they branch toward the top, giving the clusters a vaselike shape. Stems are solid or pithy, not hollow as with many grasses. They seem rough to the touch.

The leaves tend to be somewhat folded along the midrib—a marked difference from big bluestem. This species also generally lacks the dense covering of fine hairs on the leaf sheaths and on the lower part of the leaf blades that is found in big bluestem. At times, however, the leaf sheaths of little bluestem may be lightly hairy. Leaf blades are 4 to 8 inches long and usually less than ¼ inch across. Until maturity, they are light green, sometimes with a whitish bloom, as if they have been lightly powdered.

Usually the top 1 inch of each branch is a seed-bearing, spikelike raceme. The stalk of this raceme carries many hairs on the inner nodes, making the generic name especially appropriate. At each node of this raceme is a pair of spikelets, one sterile and one fertile. The sterile spikelet is short and awn-tipped; the fertile spikelet is longer and has a sharply bent and twisted awn that is longer than the spikelet itself.

The Comanche treated syphilitic sores with ashes from the stem of little bluestem.

The seeds are a common food of songbirds. The entire plant provides forage for deer, antelope, and buffalo.

A relative, broomsedge (*A. virginicus*), has been used as a dye to produce yellowish to gold to greenish yellow colors in wool.

A little bluestem prairie is colorful. It has many showy forbs because, with its shorter grasses, there is less competition for light and there is space to grow between the clumps. In the fall, hills covered with little bluestem turn a warm reddish purple.

photograph by John Schwegman

Other common names: western silvery aster, mouse-eared aster

Aster: from Greek, meaning "star," in reference to the general shape of the flower and its bracts

Sericeus: meaning "silky," referring to the soft, silky feel of the early leaves

Daisy family: Asteraceae (Compositae)

Found throughout much of temperate central North America, mostly on dry, open prairies, although it is sometimes also found in dry, open woods and on bluffs. Some people consider this dainty and modest little plant to be an indicator species for dry or sandy prairie soil. Blooms August to October.

The slender, erect, stiff, leafy stems of silky aster may be from 1 to 2 feet high but are usually less. The smooth, dark brownish red, wiry stem arises from a spreading, perennial root system. The alternate and sessile stem leaves are ½ to 1½ inches long and about ½ inch wide. Both sides of these lanceolate to oblong leaves have a dense silvery, silky pubescence that is sometimes described as resembling the soft, silky feel of a mouse's ear—the basis for one of the plant's common names.

Each of the several flower heads is about 1½ inches across and has a yellow center disk. The 15 to 25 blue to violet rays are ½ to ¾ inch long.

The *Aster* genus has at least 250 species, with possibly 200 or more occurring in North America. Many of these species also hybridize. L. H. Bailey, author of *A Standard Cyclopedia of Horticulture,* writes that the aster genus is "a large temperate-zone genus of attractive but botanically confused, mostly perennial leafy herbs particularly abundant in North America." However, the silky aster is so strikingly different that it is relatively easy to identify. The beautiful display of its cerulean blue to violet or purple flower against the background of soft, silky, silvery leaves makes the finding of this flower a special event!

The silky aster is commonly found growing in company with lead plant, little bluestem, prairie dropseed, purple prairie clover, and side oats grama grass.

Silky aster has been reported as having been used to treat arthritis. Patients were immersed in hot bath water in which the leaves, stems, and flowers of silky asters had been soaking.

photograph by Jean Novacek

Other common names: green muhly, marsh muhly

Muhlenbergia: in honor of Gotthilf Henry Ernest Muhlenberg, an American botanist of the late 18th and early 19th centuries

Racemosa: from Latin, meaning "having a raceme." (A raceme is a cluster or head of flowers, each on its own stalk and arranged along a single central stem of the flower head.)

Grass family: Poaceae (Gramineae)

Found in a wide range of prairie habitats, but it favors drier and rocky areas. Blooming time is August through September.

This sod-forming perennial grows 2 to 4 feet tall. Its stout stems have erect branches that mostly branch from the middle nodes. The internodes of the stem are smooth and shiny.

Leaf blades, ⅛ to ¼ inch across, are usually 3 to 6 inches long. The surfaces are rough and firm. The blades generally stand more or less erect along the stem.

Sheaths clasp the stem loosely. They are keeled as the midrib of the blade extends down the sheath. A collar nearly ¼ inch long is conspicuous where the blade joins the sheath.

The dense and compact seed head is usually 1 to 5 inches long and ¾ inch across. It stands erect, without the usual flexing. Typically it varies from greenish to purplish in color.

The single-flowered spikelets, which are about ¼ inch long, crowd irregularly along the flowerstalk, giving the seed head the appearance of being lobed. The glumes taper to short, stiff awns. The anthers are shorter than those of related species.

The seed grains are held tightly in the head. Shaped as tiny cylinders, they are less than ¹⁄₁₆ inch long.

This species spreads by slender, branching rhizomes that are about ⅛ inch thick and have prominent scales.

Muhly grass is an important forage grass of the plains, but some of its relatives are troublesome weeds. The more than 60 species of this large genus display a variety of growth forms ranging from erect to prostrate.

Some species in the Southwest have been used to make brushes (e.g., hairbrushes) and brooms.

photograph by Ted Van Bruggen

Other common names: common reed grass, reed, pole-reed, bog-reed, Dutch reed, wild broom-corn, spires, bennels

Phragmites: from Greek, meaning generally "growing in hedges or fencelike," apparently from the hedgelike appearance as it grows along ditches

Australis: from Latin, meaning "southern or southerly"

Grass family: Poaceae (Gramineae)

Found growing in marshes and along the banks of streams and lakeshores, often in extensive colonies. It grows worldwide; in North America, it is widely distributed, occurring across southern Canada south to California, Louisiana, and Florida. It is usually found growing amid or near cattails. Flowering begins in late August.

The stout, leafy stems of this species grow erect to as much as 16 feet tall. It seldom produces seed but spreads from an extensive network of stout, creeping rhizomes or from runners (stolons) that may extend as far as 30 feet from the point of origin.

The leaf blades tend to be wide, as much as 2 inches across, but taper to a point. Their length is usually 6 inches to 2 feet. Leaf sheaths overlap each other because they are longer than the internodes.

The large seed heads, usually 6 to 16 inches long, are tawny in color or sometimes are purplish. Most of the branches of the seed head tend to be ascending and are shorter toward the top of the seedstalk, creating a somewhat triangular-shaped seed head. Hairs on the branches of the seedstalk are longer than the individual flowers, giving the entire seed head a somewhat fuzzy appearance.

The stems of reed grass were sometimes used as shafts for arrows. The leaves were woven into mats and screens. Fibers from reed grass were used to make ropes and nets. In the Southwest, this species (along with a related exotic species, *Arundo donax*) has been used for lattices in the construction of adobe huts.

Apparently some native Americans used the grains as food. When cooked, the rootstalk served as a starchy vegetable.

When punctured, the stem exudes a pasty substance (honeydew) that hardens into a gum. This was collected and eaten as a candy. The punctured stems also were collected and the sugar was shaken off and dissolved in water to make a sweet drink.

American Indians of the Mohave Desert collected, dried, and ground the stalks into a flour. Because of its high sugar content, this flour swelled and turned brown when placed near a fire. This was then eaten like taffy.

The Yuma Indians made a cane pipe from the internodes of the stem.

photograph by Ted Van Bruggen

Other common names: barrel gentian, blind gentian, bottle gentian, cloistered gentian

Gentiana: This genus is named for the ancient King Gentius of Illyria, who supposedly discovered the medicinal properties of gentians. The gentian he knew, however, was of another genus.

Andrewsii: in honor of Henry C. Andrews, an English botanical artist and engraver of the early 19th century

Gentian family: Gentianaceae

Found throughout the tallgrass biome in wet to mesic prairies, swales, and woodland edges. Begins blooming in late August and continues past frost.

The usually unbranched stems of closed gentian are stout and leafy and grow to a height of 20 inches. They arise, usually in tufts, from a coarse, perennial root system.

The lance-shaped leaves, without petioles, are arranged in opposite pairs along the stem. The upper leaves are longer, often surpassing 4 inches. The uppermost leaves tend to form a whorl of four to six leaves at the base of the inflorescence. The margins of the leaves usually are smooth but occasionally are irregular and have a fringe of hairs.

The barrel-shaped flowers are up to 2 inches long and vary from bright blue to lighter shades of blue and rarely to white. Flowers, on short flowerstalks, are clustered in the axils of the upper leaves. Often only the very uppermost cluster has more than one or two "bottles," or flowers. The petals remain closed, joined by a whitish membrane; even when in full bloom, flowers appear more like buds that are about to open than like blossoms. The flowering of this species is one of the last colorful events on the prairie; it often blooms and persists during the time of hard frosts.

Closed gentian may be self-fertilized in most cases. Only strong and persistent bees such as bumblebees can force their way into the closed blossom and carry the pollen to another plant.

The fruit is an upright capsule that contains innumerable small seeds.

The Meskwaki and the Potawatomi used the closed gentian to treat snakebite. The women of some tribes ate a piece of root as a treatment for caked breasts. The Catawba boiled roots in water and used the liquid to treat backache.

Pioneers used the root of this species to promote appetite. Following a bout with malaria or infectious diseases, they brewed a tea from the foliage to aid digestion.

In Switzerland, a potent, alcoholic beverage called gentiane is fermented from the roots of a related species, *G. lutea.* The poorer people of Sweden used a gentian in place of hops to brew their ale.

Other gentians that grace our prairie landscape are *G. puberula,* downy gentian, with a deep purple color and folds between the corolla lobes; *G. crinita,* fringed gentian, with fringed petals and broad upper leaves; and *G. procera,* with fringed petals and narrow upper leaves.

photograph by John Schwegman

Other common names: common ladies' tresses, drooping ladies' tresses, nodding ladies' tresses, screw-auger, spike orchid, wild tuberose

Spiranthes: from Greek *speira,* meaning "a coil or spiral," from the spirally twisted flower spike

Cernua: from Latin, meaning "nodding"

Orchid family: Orchidaceae

Found in both wet and mesic prairies, in swampy areas, and occasionally in road ditches. Blooms from mid-August through September.

The stout, erect stem of ladies' tresses grows to 2 feet tall. It may be covered with fine hairs toward the top. The perennial root system has thick, fleshy branches that only descend a few inches into the soil.

Pale green, grasslike basal leaves are generally 2 to 12 inches long and about ½ inch or less in width. (The basal leaves have disappeared by the time the stems and flowers appear.) Stem leaves, which are nearly without blades, provide alternate sheathing along the stem.

Three spirals of flowers form a dense spike 2 to 6 inches long and ½ to 1 inch across. Each flower, on its own short stalk, is less than ½ inch long. The delicate flowers are ivory white. A "hood" is formed by three petal-like sepals and two lateral petals that arch upward. The fiddle-shaped "lip" (the center petal) is about

⅜ inch long and bends downward. Unlike many orchid species, these flowers have no spur.

The flowers spread outward from the flowerstalk and often droop slightly. Since they begin blooming from the bottom of the spike, it takes a few weeks before those at the top are in bloom. Flowers are sometimes fragrant, reminding one of lily-of-the-valley or of vanilla extract (which is obtained from another orchid species).

The fruit, an oval capsule about ¼ inch long, is borne more or less erect. Each seed has two or more embryos.

The Meskwaki called the plant *soa num,* meaning "tail of a rattlesnake." They did not use it as a medicine.

S. autumnales (European ladies' tresses) was used in early medicine.

The Ojibwa used the root of slender ladies' tresses, *S. gracilis,* as an ingredient in a hunting charm to bring game within range of the bow and arrow.

S. magnicamporum, Great Plains ladies' tresses, has recently been separated from *S. cernua;* it is now considered a distinct species. A plant of dry prairies, it has a distinctive scent and blooms late in the fall, often after the first frost.

photograph by Randall A. Maas

Other common names: simply "aster," although some localized common names, such as starwort or first flower, are used to designate certain species

Aster: from Greek, meaning "star," in reference to the general shape of the flower and its bracts

Species: At least 200 species are found in North America, many in the tall-, mid-, and shortgrass prairies of the Midwest. Differences between species are often minor. Some natural hybridizing also occurs. *Aster novae-angliae,* the New England aster, is shown here.

Daisy family: Asteraceae (Compositae)

Found throughout the central prairie in a wide range of habitats varying from marsh to woodlands to prairie. In addition to *A. sericeus,* the silky aster (see p. 253), other species are frequently found. These include *A. azureus, A. ericoides,* and *A. laevis* on moist soils; *A. ptarmicoides* on dry soils; *A. puniceus* and *A. umbellatus* in marsh areas; and *A. junciformis* in bogs. Asters usually grow in colonies that frequently cover large areas. Often striking in color and appearance, the flowers bloom from July through frost, mostly in late summer.

Most asters are perennials with substantial, branching root systems. A few are annuals or biennials. They generally have stout, leafy stems with numerous branches. Among the largest is the New England aster, which may grow to 4 feet tall or more if conditions are favorable.

The leaves of asters are alternate and numerous, but they vary in shape with the species. Some appear as large, pointed hearts with toothed margins and have long petioles; others are toothless, narrow, and lance-shaped and clasp the stem.

Distinctive flower heads provide identification of the genus and sometimes of the species. A single, sometimes double, set of ray florets surrounds a central disk-shaped cluster of tiny, yellow, tubular florets. The yellow disk may turn purple with age. The colorful rays provide some of nature's brightest colors—blue, purple, and sometimes shades of red.

Numerous flower heads ¼ inch to 2 inches across, depending on the species, are usually borne in loose heads near the tops of branches. New England aster's showy, purple flower head with its orange center may reach an inch across, while the white heath aster flower head is perhaps ½ inch across and resembles daisy fleabane. Asters have several circles of bracts around the flower head, while fleabane, which flowers earlier in the season, has only one.

The Ojibwa and the Chippewa used the young, fresh leaves of the big-leaf aster (*A. macrophyllus*) as greens.

Several tribes thought the smoke from burning aster plants was helpful in reviving a person who had fainted. Some tribes brewed a tea of aster plants for headaches.

The Meskwaki made a smudge from the blossoms of *A. lateriflorus* to treat insanity. They also used the large-leaf aster to treat a mother whose baby was born dead.

photograph by LeRoy G. Pratt

Abscission layer. A layer of special cells at the base of an appendage that allows the appendage to separate from the rest of the plant

Achene. A small, dry, hard, one-seeded fruit

Alterative. A substance that gradually changes a condition

Analgesic. An agent that reduces or controls pain

Anodyne. A substance that relieves pain

Anthelmintic. A substance that can expel or kill intestinal worms

Antihysteric. A substance that lessens the state of nervous instability and hysteria

Antiperiodic. A remedy that prevents the return of periodic diseases, such as certain fevers

Antirheumatic. An agent that helps to relieve pain in the joints

Antisyphilitic. A substance that supposedly relieves or controls syphilis

Aperient. A laxative

Astringent. A substance that contracts body tissue and blood vessels, checking the flow of blood

Awn. A slender, bristle-shaped appendage; usually used in describing grasses

Bifid. Forked; divided by a cleft

Biome. Large, easily recognizable community units, e.g., the grassland biome

Bract. A modified leaf subtending a flower or flower cluster

Callus. A hard protuberance; in grasses, a tough swelling at the point of insertion of the palea and lemma

Calyx. The sepals of a flower, considered collectively

Carminative. A substance that relieves gas and colic

Carpel. A simple pistil, or one member of a compound pistil

Cholagogue. A substance that increases the flow of bile

Ciliate. Marginally fringed with hairs

Claw. The narrowed base of some sepals and petals

Corolla. The collection of petals of a flower

Culm. The stem of a grass or sedge

Cyme. A cluster of flowers in which each main and secondary stem bears a single flower

Decoction. An extract produced by boiling a substance in water

Dentate. With pointed teeth, as with the margins of leaves

Diaphoretic. A substance that increases the flow of perspiration

Diuretic. A substance that increases the flow of urine

Emmenagogue. A substance that induces menstrual flow

Epispastic. A substance that produces blistering

Escharotic. Tending to produce a dry scab resulting from a burn or corrosive substance

Expectorant. A substance that causes mucous to be expelled from the respiratory tract

Glabrous. Smooth, without hairs or glands

Glume. The husk or chafflike bract of grasses

Heterogeneous. Differing or opposite in structure or quality

Indehiscent. Remaining closed at maturity

Inflorescence. The flower cluster of a plant

Infusion. A substance made by steeping a plant material in a liquid without boiling

Laciniate. With a torn appearance

Lemma. The lower of the two bracts enclosing the flower of a grass

Ligule. The small growth on a grass where the blade meets the culm

Mesic. The part of a prairie that is neither excessively wet or dry

Moxa. A soft, woolly mass prepared from stems and used as a cautery by burning it on the skin; a substance similarly used

Nauseant. A substance that produces nausea

Obovate. Having the shape of the longitudinal section of an egg, with the broad end at the top

Palea. The inner of a pair of bracts enclosing a grass flower

Panicle. A branched, compound inflorescence

Pappus. A crown of bristles, or hairs, on the seed, which aids in dissemination

Pedicel. The stalk of a flower in a flower cluster

Peduncle. The stem of a group of flowers or of a single flower, if only one is present

Petiole. The stalk or stem of a leaf

Pinna. A primary division (leaflet) of a pinnately compound leaf

Pistil. The female flower parts: stigma, style, and ovary

Propagule. A runner or sucker used in asexual reproduction of plants

Pubescent. Covered with very fine, soft hairs

Purgative. A substance that causes bowel movement; cathartic

Raceme. An elongate flower cluster with short lateral branches that bear the individual flowers

Rachis. The axis of a leaf or an inflorescence

Rhizome. An underground stem

Rubefacient. A substance that produces irritation and reddening of the skin

Sepal. One of the leaflike parts of the calyx

Sessile. Without a stem

Spasmodic. Characterized by sudden and intermittent spasms

Spike. An elongate flower cluster with sessile individual flowers

Spikelet. The ultimate flower cluster in grasses and sedges

Stamen. The male portion of the flower: anther (pollen sac) and filament

Standard. The upper, usually broad petal of the flowers of the Legume family

Stipules. Leaflike appendages at the base of the petiole

Stolon. An elongate stem on the surface of the soil

Styptic. A substance that shrinks blood vessels, slowing or stopping blood loss

Taxon (pl. taxa). A taxonomic entity, regardless of size or rank

Terete. Circular in cross section; columnar

Tomentose. Densely pubescent, often appearing like matted wool

Umbel. A flower arrangement where a number of flowerstalks that are nearly equal in length spread from a common center

Vulnerary. A substance that promotes healing of open wounds

Xeric. The driest part of a site or area, especially prairies

Angier, B. 1978. Field guide to medicinal wild plants. Harrisburg, Pa.: Stackpole Books.

Bailey, L. H. 1963. The standard cyclopedia of horticulture. New York: Macmillan.

Bedell, T. D. 1983. Nuclear reactions? *Horticulture* 61(6)22–23.

Conard, H. S. 1951. Plants of Iowa. 7th ed. of the Grinnell Flora, Grinnell College, Grinnell, Iowa. Published by the author.

Coon, N. 1974. The dictionary of useful plants. Erasmus, Pa.: Rodale.

Deam, C. C. 1940. Flora of Indiana. Indianapolis: Indiana Dept. of Conservation.

Denison, E. 1972. Missouri wildflowers. Springfield: Missouri Dept. of Conservation.

Densmore, F. 1974. How Indians use wild plants for food, medicine, and crafts. New York: Dover.

Elliott, D. 1976. Roots: An underground botany and forager's guide. Old Greenwich, Conn.: Chatham Press.

Fernald, M. L. 1950. Gray's manual of botany. New York: Van Nostrand.

Fernald, M. L., and A. C. Kinsey. 1958. Edible wild plants of eastern North America. Revised by R. C. Rollins. New York: Harper.

Fielder, M. 1975. Plant medicine and folklore. New York: Winchester Press.

Gilmore, M. R. 1977. Uses of plants by the Indians of the Missouri River region. Lincoln: Univ. of Nebraska Press.

Gleason, H. A. 1968. The new Britton and Brown illustrated flora of the northeastern United States and adjacent Canada. New York: Hafner.

Hedrick, V. P., ed. 1919. Sturdevant's edible plants of the world. New York: Dover.

Hitchcock, A. S. 1951. Manual of the grasses of the United States. 2d ed. Revised by A. Chase. Washington, D.C.: U.S.D.A. Publication 200.

Kingsbury, J. M. 1964. Poisonous plants of the United States and Canada. Englewood Cliffs, N.J.: Prentice-Hall.

Krochmal, A., and C. Krochmal. 1973. A guide to medicinal wild plants. New York: New York Times Book Co.

Lommaasson, R. C. 1973. Nebraska wildflowers. Lincoln: Univ. of Nebraska Press.

Madson, J. 1982. Where the sky began: Land of the tallgrass prairie. Boston: Houghton Mifflin.

Medsger, O. P. 1957. Edible wild plants. New York: Macmillan.

Miller, H. 1983. Tradescantia. *Horticulture* 61(6):20–21.

Millspaugh, C. 1974. American medicinal plants. New York: Dover.

Mohlenbrock, R. 1975. Guide to the vascular plants of Illinois. Carbondale: Southern Illinois Univ. Press.

Muenscher, W. C. 1957. Poisonous plants of the United States and Canada. New York: Macmillan.

Newcomb, L. 1977. Newcomb's wildflower guide. Boston: Little, Brown.

Owensby, C. E. 1980. Kansas prairie wildflowers. Ames: Iowa State Univ. Press.

Palmer, E. L., and H. S. Fowler. 1975. Fieldbook of natural history. New York: McGraw-Hill.

Peterson, L. 1978. A guide to edible wild plants. Boston: Houghton Mifflin.

Peterson, R. T., and M. McKenna. 1968. A field guide to wildflowers of northeast and north central North America. Boston: Houghton Mifflin.

Phillips Petroleum Company. 1963. Pasture and range plants. Bartlesville, Okla.

Rickett, H. W. 1965. Wildflowers of the United States. New York: McGraw-Hill.

Risser, P. G., E. C. Birney, H. D. Blocker, S. W. May, W. J. Parton, and J. A. Wiens. 1981. The true prairie ecosystem. Stroudsburg, Pa.: Hutchinson Ross.

Rogers, D. J. 1980. Edible, medicinal, useful, and poisonous wild plants of the Northern Great Plains, South Dakota region. Sioux Falls, S.D.: Biology Dept., Augustana College.

Runkel, S. T., and A. F. Bull. 1979/1987. Wildflowers of Iowa woodlands. Ames: Iowa State University Press.

Sievers, A. F. 1930. American medicinal plants of commercial importance. Washington, D.C.: U.S.D.A. Publication 77.

Smith, H. H. 1923. Ethnobotany of the Menomini. Milwaukee, Wis.: Bulletin of the Milwaukee Public Museum.

_____. 1928. Ethnobotany of the Meskwaki Indians. Milwaukee, Wis.: Bulletin of the Milwaukee Public Museum.

_____. 1932. Ethnobotany of the Ojibwe. Milwaukee, Wis.: Bulletin of the Milwaukee Public Museum.

_____. 1933. Ethnobotany of the Forest Potawatomi. Milwaukee, Wis.: Bulletin of the Milwaukee Public Museum.

Steyermark, J. A. 1968. Flora of Missouri. Ames: Iowa State Univ. Press.

Transeau, E. N. 1935. The prairie peninsula. *Ecology* 16:423–37.

Van Bruggen, T. 1976. Wildflowers of the northern plains and Black Hills. Bulletin no. 3, Badlands Natural History Assoc., Interior, S.Dak.

274